What has Infant Baptism done to Baptism?
An enquiry at the end of Christendom

Didsbury Lectures, 2003

What has Infant Baptism done to Baptism?

An enquiry at the end of Christendom

David F. Wright

Copyright © 2005 David F. Wright

First published in 2005 by Paternoster Press

10 09 08 07 06 05   7 6 5 4 3 2 1

Paternoster Press is an imprint of Authentic Media,
9 Holdom Avenue, Bletchley, Milton Keynes MK1 1QR, UK
and
129 Mobilization Drive, Waynesboro, GA 30830-4575, USA

www.authenticmedia.co.uk/paternoster

The right of David F. Wright to be identified as the Author of this Work has been asserted by him in accordance with the Copyright, Designs and Patents Act 1988.

All rights reserved. No part of this publication may be reproduced, stored in a retrieval system, or transmitted in any form or by any means, electronic, mechanical, photocopying, recording or otherwise, without the prior permission of the publisher or a licence permitting restricted copying. In the UK such licences are issued by the Copyright Licensing Agency, 90 Tottenham Court Road, London W1P 9HE.

British Library Cataloguing in Publication Data
A catalogue record for this book is available from the British Library

ISBN 1-84227-357-4

Unless otherwise stated, Scripture quotations are taken from the
HOLY BIBLE, NEW INTERNATIONAL VERSION
Copyright © 1973, 1978, 1984 by the International Bible Society.

Used by permission of Hodder and Stoughton Limited.
All rights reserved.

'NIV' is a registered trademark of the International Bible Society.
UK trademark number 1448790.

Cover Design by fourninezero design.
Typeset by WestKey Ltd, Falmouth, Cornwall
Print Management by Adare Carwin
Printed and Bound by J.H. Haynes & Co., Sparkford

Contents

Foreword by Tony Lane	vii
Acknowledgements	ix
Introduction	1
1. Infant Baptism in the Hands of Christendom	11
2. Baptism and Profession of Faith: What? Whose?	35
3. Baptism in Mission: Catechumenate and Discipleship	63
4. Baptism: Effective Sign, or Merely Symbolic?	83
Bibliography	103
Biblical Index	109
Modern Author Index	111
General Index	113

Foreword

This book is not David Wright's first engagement with the issue of baptism. I personally know of (and have read) at least twenty of his earlier, shorter pieces on this topic, written over some twenty years. The present volume builds on the solid research and scholarship of the earlier works.

One of the good developments of the last century is the fact that most Christians are now much more willing to be critical of their own traditions. David Wright writes as one from within the paedobaptist tradition, from a national church that practises widespread if not indiscriminate infant baptism, and he is highly critical of this tradition. By the end of the volume the reader will be thoroughly acquainted with the harmful effects that this practice has had and its failure at the present time to turn people into practising Christians or even churchgoers. This (to quote the subtitle) 'enquiry at the end of Christendom' forcefully points to the failure of infant baptism to 'deliver the goods' in today's world, whatever may have been its effectiveness in the past.

These lectures are highly critical of the contemporary practice of infant baptism, but it would be a mistake to conclude that they simply support the Baptist cause, for two reasons. First, the practice being discussed and criticised is the 'universal baptizing of babies' that took place under Christendom and supplanted the practice of believers' baptism. This should be distinguished from the situation in the early centuries where the two forms of baptism existed side by side, both because of the large influx of converts and because by no means all Christians brought their babies to baptism. The 'dual practice' of allowing Christians the choice of whether or not to have their children baptized, and if so at what age, may strike many today as muddled and unprincipled – but the clear fact is that such a variety of practice existed in the third and fourth centuries and that no one raised any principled objection against it. Indeed, it can be argued from this fact that it is most likely that such acceptance of variety goes back to apostolic times.[1]

Secondly, while infant baptism may be in a mess at 'the end of Christendom', all is not well on the other side. Most (but by no means all) Baptists have reduced baptism to a merely symbolic event by which they testify to their own faith. This is unfaithful both to the New Testament and to the teaching of the Reformers, as is spelt out in the final chapter of this book. The 'universal baptizing of babies' is not the only way to distort Scripture. Until evangelicals take seriously the clear teaching of the New Testament about the efficacy of baptism, they cannot expect those of other traditions to take them seriously on this topic.

It has become widely accepted that the basis for any future consensus will be the recognition of believers' baptism as the normative form of baptism (the default setting, one might say) and of infant baptism as an acceptable variation from that norm. The present volume greatly contributes to that goal by decisively deconstructing the old myths about the validity and efficacy of the 'universal baptizing of babies'.

Tony Lane
London School of Theology

---

[1] As I have argued in, 'Did the Apostolic Church Baptise Babies? A Seismological Approach', *Tyndale Bulletin* 55.1 (May 2004), 109–30.

Acknowledgements

The four chapters that make up this slim book were delivered as the Didsbury Lectures for 2003 in the J.B. Maclagan Chapel of the Nazarene Theological College, Didsbury, Manchester, during 27–30 October 2003. My first vote of thanks must be to the Faculty of the College for inviting me to lecture in this series. Since the lectureship was inaugurated by the late Professor F.F. Bruce in 1979, its growing prestige has enhanced the standing of the College – and vice versa. I recognize the honour done to me by the teaching body of the College and express my warm appreciation.

My wife Anne-Marie and I were right royally fed and entertained during the week of the lectures in Didsbury. For the solicitude and generosity of their hospitality, we were indebted to the College community as a whole and especially to Principal Herbert McGonigle (whose withdrawal through illness halfway through the series had nothing to do, I trust, with the initial lectures), Dr Kent Brower, who, with his successor as Dean, Dr Peter Rae, set most of the arrangements in place, Professor Tom Noble, former student of mine in Edinburgh and long-time collaborator in the task of patristic and evangelical theology, Dr David Rainey and Dr Dwight Swanson. Nor do Anne-Marie and I forget the many kindnesses of their several wives. The College Registrar, Alison Yarwood, was helpful in many practical ways. It was for us a memorable week.

Finally, my thanks are due also to Fay Binnie, who turned my handwriting into an inerrant typescript while I still hesitated to embrace that *mysterium* more *tremendum* than *fascinans*, the computer.

Introduction

The history of Christian baptism remains a somewhat neglected field of study, particularly when it comes to its development from the beginning to the present day viewed as a whole. Maxwell E. Johnson makes this point in the introduction to the book by which he seeks to fill the lacuna, *The Rites of Christian Initiation: Their Evolution and Interpretation* (Collegeville, MN: Liturgical Press, 1999). He has given us a scholarly one-volume account covering the whole span of baptismal history – a niche which it occupies almost unrivalled in English-language publications. Yet the book's Catholic provenance and interest, its strong focus on baptismal ritual and the inclusion of confirmation (and also first communion) within its scope will not promote its widespread use in some significant circles in theological education.

Beyond English, the remarkable compilation by Jules Corblet, *Histoire dogmatique, liturgique et archéologique du sacrement de baptême* (2 Vols; Paris: Victor Palmé, 1881–82) remains untranslated and largely unknown. Although in comprehensiveness it stands almost unchallenged, then or since, the dogmatic interest is largely Catholic and the author's expertise in matters ceremonial and external holds centre stage. In German, two massive essays by Georg Kretschmar and Bruno Jordahn in *Der Taufgottesdienst*, volume 5 of *Leiturgia: Handbuch des*

Evangelischen Gottesdienstes (ed. K.F. Müller and W. Blankenburg; Kassel: Johannes Stauda-Verlag, 1970), deal respectively with the early church (pp. 1–348) and the period from the Middle Ages to the twentieth century (pp. 349–640). Together they give the best scholarly overall treatment of the subject. They too, however, remain inaccessible to most of the Anglophone world. The much older German two-volume work by Johann Wilhelm Friedrich Höfling, *Das Sakrament der Taufe nebst den anderen damit zusammenhängenden Akten der Initiation* (Erlangen: Palm'sche Verlagsbuchhandlung, 1846–48), provides over a thousand unindexed pages of dogmatic, historical and liturgical study, with a strong Lutheran interest in the sixteenth to eighteenth centuries. A work in English commonly regarded as a classic, William Wall's *The History of Infant Baptism*, in two volumes first published in 1705, offers less than its title promises, being confined to the early centuries and later controversies about their evidence.

I am not forgetting the ample stream of works on particular periods of baptism's history, especially on the patristic centuries. Yet a synoptic view of its fortunes in the Reformation era is still lacking, and the modern world is even more thinly covered. Among a host of specialized studies Peter Cramer's *Baptism and Change in the Early Middle Ages, c. 200 – c. 1150* (Cambridge: Cambridge University Press, 1993) is notable in plotting momentous transitions in the practice and understanding of baptism. More analyses of this kind and scope will undoubtedly pave the way to an overall history of baptism.

Why baptism should have fared so much more poorly than the Lord's supper is patient of a variety of explanations, some of which will be found scattered through these Didsbury Lectures. One inescapable reason is that the early history of baptism remains strongly contested. Indeed, at the outset of the twenty-first century, students of the church of the Fathers no longer line up harmoniously behind the consensus which has in broad terms prevailed since the sixteenth century and was in the recent past expansively represented by Joachim Jeremias's *Infant Baptism in the First Four Centuries* (London: SCM Press, 1960; German original, 1958). Before a fresh account can emerge to win wide assent, closer attention will have to be paid to the fourth century, when the baptism of the newborn became at best marginal. Understanding what happened then may prove more helpful in clarifying earlier developments than another dozen investigations of household baptisms in the New Testament.

Yet if it is difficult to write a history of baptism while agreement is lacking whether its earliest development encompassed infants, generally, more selectively or not at all, the post-patristic story seems by contrast much more straightforward. Infant baptism became regnant, and the millennium or so up to the Reformation witnessed only popular, small-scale, uncoordinated and short-lived protests in favour of baptism for believers only. The Protestant Reformers had their quarrels with the Roman Catholic Church over the import, and minor aspects of the practice, of infant baptism, but these were scarcely comparable in magnitude to their polemic against the mass as a wholesale perversion of Christ's supper. The Reformers inherited and transmitted almost completely intact the doctrine traditional since the fourth century that a layperson could validly baptize, so that the ministry of baptism never attracted controversies over priesthood, ordination and apostolic succession which exacerbated discord about the Lord's supper itself – and have continued to divide churches of Reformation lineage until the modern day.[1] Nor was there any equivalent in respect of baptism to the 'supper-strife' which so deeply vitiated the unity of the Reformation.

When the Anabaptist protest emerged, its impact by reaction upon the mainstream Reformation movements was – so we must judge, with the benefit of hindsight – largely detrimental. The Old Church and the new Protestantism – the new papalism alongside the old, as the Anabaptists read it – joined ranks in suppressing the dissenters. The contemporary church still waits for appropriate acknowledgement by the Vatican and the worldwide Anglican and Reformed communions (the Lutherans of Germany have in good measure led the way and the Swiss Reformed churches have followed more recently) of their forbears' scandalous mistreatment of the first significant modern advocates of long-lost dimensions of New Testament baptism.

One legacy of the baptismal breach of the sixteenth century which has militated against a comprehensive history of baptism has been the stubborn hauteur displayed

---

[1] The contrast is only too evident within the first canon of the Fourth Lateran Council of 1215. Whereas 'none can effect this sacrament [of the eucharist] except the priest who has been rightly ordained in accordance with the keys of the church which Jesus Christ Himself granted to the Apostles and their successors', baptism can be '[d]uly conferred on both infants and adults by any one at all in the form appointed by the church'; John H. Leith (ed.), *Creeds of the Churches* (Richmond, VA: John Knox Press, 1973²), 58. Dr Graham Keith brought to my attention a remarkable nineteenth-century development in Scottish Highland piety which distinguished between an 'uncontradicted' profession of faith required for admission to baptism and an 'accredited' profession demanded for the Lord's supper. This meant that 'the Church ought to sustain, in the case of a person applying for baptism *either for himself* or for his child, *a profession not made incredible by ignorance and immorality*', in contrast to the careful examination of life and experience engaged in prior to the supper. Cf. John Kennedy, *The Days of the Fathers in Rossshire* (enlarged edn; Inverness: 'Northern Chronicle' Office, 1897), 143, cf. 140–48 (my italics).

Introduction 5

towards Baptists and believers' baptism by paedobaptist churches and theologians. A friend recalls a world-famous Scottish Reformed theologian telling a seminar in the 1970s that Baptist teaching was 'a bit of a theological slum'. Writing in 1966, the late George R. Beasley-Murray, whose *Baptism in the New Testament* (London: Macmillan & Co., 1962) now stands as a landmark in the modern scholarly *retractatio* of early Christian baptism, reported as follows:

> In our own time I find that a Lutheran pastor, when attacking a fellow-Lutheran who had the temerity to question infant baptism, pointed out that it was the Anabaptists who were responsible for this heretical teaching, and that their own forefathers had judged their views so seriously as to demand the death penalty for them; the spirit of his article conveyed the impression that it was unfortunate that the same penalty could not be exacted today! Even now, in the more tolerant atmosphere of ecumenical conversation, it is possible for a Baptist in a discussion group to create an uproar if he has the temerity to express candidly his views on Christian initiation.[2]

Even today, a full generation later, a critical reading of the paedobaptist case does not everywhere receive a fair hearing. A colleague in Germany sent me recently the text of a *Habilitationsvorlesung* on 'Theological Problems of Infant Baptism' presented by a strongly Lutheran candidate before a Protestant Theological Faculty in Germany. The text was subjected to severe criticism from Faculty members.

A credible history of baptism, at least so far as Western Christianity is concerned, can be told only if the overwhelming domination of the tradition by infant baptism is

---
[2] George R. Beasley-Murray, *Baptism Today and Tomorrow* (London: MacMillan, 1966), 112–13.

subjected to searching scrutiny. Contributing to that task is one of the major aims of this set of four lectures. The monopoly enjoyed by paedobaptism has too often obscured diversity of practice and also interaction, even if only by way of reaction, between different forms of baptism. Peter Leithart has recently asserted that 'The church was rescued from Baptist theology and practice by Augustine of Hippo.'[3] If 'Baptist' here implies rejection of infant baptism, this wonderfully bold statement is an exaggeration but within pardonable limits.[4] (Let no one think of Donatism in this connexion; its offence had nothing to do with the difference between infant and faith-professing baptism.) To Leithart '[t]he remarkable fact about baptism in the early church is that infant baptism emerged ... as the dominant practice of the church'.[5] This is not the way the story is usually told! It is indeed seriously misleading to view the age of the Fathers simply as an era of infant baptism. In fact, of known named individuals in those centuries who were both of Christian parentage and baptized at known dates, the great majority were baptized on profession of faith. The obscuring of a truer picture derives ultimately from sixteenth-century apologetic, both Catholic and Protestant, against the Anabaptists.

It was, with minor exceptions, not until the later twentieth century that churches began again to experience what must have obtained at least until Augustine's time – the coexistence of both forms of baptism (perhaps more than two!) within one communion. Today we talk of dual-practice or equivalent-alternatives baptismal regimes. It is

---

[3] Peter Leithart, 'Infant Baptism in History: An Unfinished Tragicomedy', in Gregg Strawbridge (ed.), *The Case for Covenantal Infant Baptism* (Phillipsburg, NJ: P&R Publishing, 2003), 246–62, at 258.

[4] See my essay, 'Augustine and the Transformation of Baptism', in Alan Kreider (ed.), *The Origins of Christendom in the West* (Edinburgh, New York: T&T Clark, 2001), 287–310.

[5] Leithart, 'Infant Baptism in History', 258.

true, of course, that no paedobaptist church has ever rejected the propriety of faith baptism for converts of responsible years. Yet for generations most such churches had little awareness of believers' baptism. If they did encounter it, it was as a rite reduced as far as possible to the dimensions of baby baptism. This was part of the price paid for the universal sway of infant baptism, as these lectures will illustrate.

Did the two patterns of baptismal initiation call for different theologies of baptism? According to Leithart again, Augustine 'treats infant and adult baptism as closely parallel in meaning and effect'.[6] John Chrysostom and other Greek Fathers made more of a distinction between the two.

The story of developments in the West is not a tidy one. The Reformers, after some initial hesitations, maintained the practice of baptizing babies but declined the traditional rationale for it bequeathed by Augustine. For him, newborn babies had to be baptized in order to escape from the guilt of original sin and its entail, eternal damnation. Since Augustine earlier in his career had been uncertain why babies should be baptized, he may be said to have eventually applied to baby baptism what he knew to be true of older candidates, who were baptized for the remission of sin. By the Reformation and its aftermath, the compass of baptismal theology had swung right round, so that what could sensibly be predicated of infant subjects came to determine theologies of baptism. This was understandable when baptisms of believers were so exceptional, but it was not excusable, for it stood the logic of baptismal evolution on its head. If vital contact had been maintained with the New Testament, the limitations of babies could never have been allowed to prescribe what was to be taught and believed about baptism.

---

[6] Ibid., 259.

The most astonishing fact about the strange history of infant baptism which these lectures explore lies in the field of liturgy. There is precious little evidence in patristic sources of services of baptism being tailored to suit the capacity of infant recipients. As Leithart helpfully summarizes, 'the earliest baptismal liturgies ... were constructed on something like Baptist assumptions, even when children were included'.[7] Yet it still strikes us as amazing that, long after paedobaptism had become universal practice in the West, infants were baptized in a ritual designed for persons able to speak for others, even to the extent that infants were 'made' to give all the appropriate responses through the mouth of parents, sponsors or priests.[8] It was as though paedobaptism had the strength of a cuckoo to eject the original occupants of the nest and thus effect a takeover of baptism, but lacked the independent vitality to fledge its own appropriate liturgical feathers. The confusing consequences for baptismal services have still not been completely flushed out of the churches' systems. The Church of England marked the millennium in 2000 by issuing its new prayer book, *Common Worship*. Its modern service of baptism requires parents, godparents and sponsors to answer in the first person singular questions addressed to babies through them. Thus they speak for the infants when they answer 'I reject ... I renounce ... I repent ... turn to, submit to, come to Christ.' This may seem to

---

[7] Ibid., 251. Leithart fails to draw the obvious conclusion from this evidence, that infant baptism can never have been the norm in this early period.

[8] Cf. P. Cramer, *Baptism and Change in the Early Middle Ages c.200 – c.1150* (Cambridge: Cambridge University Press, 1993), 3: 'Thus one of the great questions raised by the history of baptism is how it was that even after the habit of infant baptism had become widespread in the churches of Latin Christendom, the *form* of adult baptism – of a rite of conversion celebrated either at Easter or Pentecost, and not just of passive or magical exorcism – continued largely to prevail.'

bespeak either an incurable antiquarianism or a flight from reality, but it is most charitably interpreted as an attempt to preserve the unity of baptism (older candidates are asked the same questions directly) and to express what recent baptismal theology across the churches has recognized, that answering-for-oneself baptism is in an appropriate sense the norm. It nevertheless represents a failure to devise a baptismal order appropriate to non-responding children. The modern Roman Catholic rite does it much better, and the Anglican form of proxy response is now an isolated relic among paedobaptist churches.

These lectures make no claim to offer even a sketch of the history of baptism in the West. Rather, they examine one fairly constant thread in that history, the damaging ascendancy of infant baptism in practice and theology since the late patristic and early medieval centuries. They do so at a time in the history of Christianity often characterized as the dying days of Christendom. Universal infant baptism was one of the constitutive elements of the unitary world of church-state Christianity which is what Christendom commonly denotes. As that pattern of the Christian society dissolves, it is important to know whether all will be lost if infant baptism also dwindles.

Away from the erstwhile citadels of Christendom in Europe, Christianity is expanding rapidly in Africa, much of Asia and Latin America. This new Christianity of the South and the East is heavily dominated by models of Christian life, old and new, which generally baptize only converts. Pentecostalism is perhaps the predominant paradigm, expressed in many highly diverse forms, of the thriving Christianity of the South. This seismic shift in the distribution of world Christianity is one of the contexts promoting a reconsideration of baptismal history today.

An historical revisiting of what has often appeared an intractable division between Christian traditions can take place early in the third millennium amid several signs of hope. These range from the stimulus given to rapprochement by the landmark Faith and Order text *Baptism, Eucharist and Ministry* (1982) and follow-up discussions, the growing evidence of sacramental thinking among Baptist theologians and the increasing adoption of dual-practice church polities, to the highly significant developments in the Catholic Church since Vatican II, exemplified in its impressive *Rite of Christian Initiation of Adults*, and the inescapable emergence among major paedobaptist communions, including the Catholic and Anglican, of a consensus which holds faith baptism as the norm with which infant baptism must be coordinated.

It is indeed a hopeful and invigorating time to engage in a re-examination of baptismal roots and traditions.

1

Infant Baptism in the Hands of Christendom

The title of this series of lectures deserves some explanation. It has been carefully worded, in part to imply clearly that infant baptism is taken seriously as a form of Christian baptism. Had it been the intention to treat it otherwise, as set over against baptism, it would have been easy enough to refer to it by some phrase which did not include the word 'baptism'.

At the same time, the overall title of the lectures should leave little doubt that their subject matter might be summarized as the problematics of infant baptism, viewed historically in the main. Such an investigation finds much of its integrity from accepting infant baptism as baptism, and not as a wholly mistaken practice which should never have been invented in the first place.

The exercise receives added seriousness from the fact that infant baptism has been the dominant form of baptism for most of Christian history throughout the world. In the sixteenth century Martin Luther liked to challenge the Anabaptists (who rejected paedobaptism) to say whether they accepted that there had been no Christian baptism for some 1500 years and consequently no Christian church. It was much more than a cheap debating point. We will return to some of its implications in due course. For the present, it provides a helpful cue for a fuller spelling out of my aim in these lectures.

Under examination will be the effects on baptism of the long reign of infant baptism as the prevalent and almost exclusive form of the sacrament for approximately a millennium and a half. The focus will be largely on the West, not on the Eastern world of Orthodoxy, and hence on European Christianity, and its European-type worldwide derivatives. The timescale of infant baptism's long reign extends from the early medieval period, from about the sixth century, that is to say, after Augustine of Hippo, who died in 430. It was he who provided the theology that led to infant baptism becoming general practice for the first time in the history of the church, perhaps in the later fifth century, more likely in the 500s or even later.

This universal baptizing of babies formed one of the building blocks of Christendom, by which I mean that long phase of Christian history during which the church and the civil order, whether people, nation or empire, were largely coterminous. Human society consisted of a single population viewed from one angle as the Christian church, from another as a state. Characteristic of Christendom was the state church, the church legally 'established' or recognized as the privileged church of the nation or empire. Christendom began to develop under the earliest Christian emperors of Rome, from Constantine in the early fourth century onwards, and survived the disruption of the Reformation largely unscathed. The re-formed churches which came out of the Reformation were state churches or national churches, whether Lutheran, Reformed or Presbyterian, or Anglican.

At times within Christendom the baptism of the newborn was required by the law of the state, as happened in the Reformation strongholds of Strasbourg and Geneva, for example. A relic of such legal prescription is the right of parents in England to have their infants baptized in the Church of England. Anglican clergy can resort to various measures to persuade unchurched parents not to have their children baptized, but in the end parents can insist on their right. In Sweden, although the links between the Lutheran church and the state were recently loosened, a very high percentage of babies are still baptized in that church, as almost an essential ceremony in their registration within the civil community.

The enquiry to be pursued in these lectures is timely for two reasons in particular. In the first place, we are living through the disintegration of Christendom. This macro-social, -political, and -cultural change has been underway in Europe for many decades, perhaps since the French Revolution of 1789. It has so many faces and dimensions that in this context it can be referred to only in general terms. The shell of Christendom – constitutional establishment of the church, as in England, or national recognition, as in Scotland – may live on long after majority allegiance to the church among the populace has been lost. On the other hand, in the USA, which is constitutionally committed to the separation of church and state, Christianity enjoys far greater acceptance and influence in national life than in more secularized Europe. Karl Barth used to argue that infant baptism belonged to the era of Christendom in the church's history. He believed that in his day the dissolution of Christendom was in train, although this was not the reason why he became the most eminent theological opponent of paedobaptism in the twentieth century.[1]

---

[1] See Karl Barth, *The Teaching of the Church Regarding Baptism* (trans. Ernest A. Payne; London: SCM, 1948) and *Church Dogmatics*, Vol. IV/4 (trans. G.W. Bromiley; Edinburgh: T & T Clark, 1969). By the time he wrote the latter, Barth regarded his earlier booklet as 'outdated from my own standpoint' (ix).

The second reason why this subject is timely belongs not to the socio-political context but to baptism itself. A significant theological shift is taking place in the direction of an acknowledgement that the norm of baptism is faith baptism. Such a statement calls for careful explication, for it must immediately be made clear that this acknowledgement does not entail the rejection or abandonment of baptizing babies. It is particularly discernible in ecumenical discussion, prompted to a considerable extent by the hugely influential Faith and Order Report from the World Council of Churches, *Baptism, Eucharist and Ministry* (1982), perhaps the most widely studied ecumenical text of the twentieth century. The recognition of faith baptism – shorthand here for baptism on personal profession of faith – as the baptismal norm, which is in good measure a summary of the New Testament witness to baptism, is firmly grounded in the Roman Catholic and Anglican communions, and is gaining acceptance in a growing number of other mainstream paedobaptist churches, including even and most recently the Church of Scotland, which had remained the most 'fundamentalist' of baby-baptizing churches. In all of these churches infant baptism is likely to remain the common or commoner practice for the foreseeable future, yet this large-scale change in baptismal theology now in process is not without real substance. What does it entail?

I will summarize a handful of points fairly briefly, since we will subsequently return to most of them from other angles. The big shift implies a movement in theological reflection *from* faith baptism *to* the baptism of infants. The starting point is important and is no longer, as in so much of the tradition, the assumption of infant baptism. There is a modest illustration of the fresh approach in the report on baptism approved by the General Assembly of the Church of Scotland in May, 2003.² The liturgical fruit of such a revised perspective on baptism is the precedence given in services of baptism to dealing with candidates who are able to answer for themselves. This is clearly seen in the Church of England's latest prayer book, *Common Worship* of 2000. It was already evident in the same church's *Alternative Service Book* of 1980.

That some devaluation of infant baptism is implicit in the shift is undeniable, even if it is not often spelt out. This is, I judge, a consequence of taking with greater seriousness the New Testament, rather than the Old Testament, in considering a theology of baptism, since traditional defences of paedobaptism have leaned heavily on the parallel with circumcision. Beyond doubt historical claims for infant baptism as current in the apostolic churches now tend to be more modest. The statement in *Baptism, Eucharist and Ministry* (hereafter referred to as *BEM*) is highly judicious:

> While the possibility that infant baptism was practised in the apostolic age cannot be excluded, baptism upon personal profession of faith is the most clearly attested pattern in the New Testament documents.[3]

A similarly qualified comment appears in the recent *Catechism of the Catholic Church* (1994):

> The practice of infant Baptism is an immemorial tradition of the Church. There is explicit testimony to this practice from the second century on, and it is quite possible that, from the beginning of the apostolic preaching, when whole 'house-

---

[2] *General Assembly 2003* (Edinburgh: Church of Scotland Board of Practice and Procedure, 2003), 13/1–13/17.

[3] *Baptism, Eucharist and Ministry* (Faith and Order Paper 111; Geneva: World Council of Churches, 1982), 4.

holds' received Baptism, infants may also have been baptized.[4]

The former of these two judgements, in *BEM*, accentuates the doubt more heavily, and would meet with widespread endorsement among New Testament scholars.

A final entailment of the movement in baptismal thinking is the encouragement of a transition in church practice towards recognition of both patterns of baptism as 'equivalent alternatives', as is the case in the Nazarene Church.[5] Most of the dual-practice churches reached that position by being unions of paedobaptist and faith-baptist churches, or more loosely by embracing communities of divergent traditions, as in the American Evangelical Covenant Church.[6] In the present ecumenical climate, which has on baptism favoured the 'baptist' stance more obviously than the paedobaptist, infant-baptizing churches have been here and there moving towards initially an informal 'dual-practice' policy by officially

---

[4] *Catechism of the Catholic Church* (London: Geoffrey Chapman, 1994), 284.

[5] The Church of the Nazarene's position on baptism is stated as follows in its *Manual 2001–2005* (Kansas City, MO: Nazarene Publishing House, 2002), 32–33: 'We believe that Christian baptism, commanded by our Lord, is a sacrament signifying acceptance of the benefits of the atonement of Jesus Christ, to be administered to believers and declarative of their faith in Jesus Christ as their Savior, and full purpose of obedience in holiness and righteousness. Baptism being a symbol of the new covenant, young children may be baptized, upon request of parents or guardians who shall give assurance for them of necessary Christian training. Baptism may be administered by sprinkling, pouring, or immersion, according to the choice of the applicant.' Cf. Jack Ford, *In the Steps of John Wesley: The Church of the Nazarene in Britain* (Kansas City, MO: Nazarene Publishing House, 1968), 193–95.

[6] On this church's changing stance on baptism (its origins are in Swedish Lutheranism) see the articles in *Covenant Quarterly* 53:4 (Nov. 1995) and 54:1 (Feb. 1996). I am grateful to Tom Noble for knowledge of this source.

acknowledging the propriety of parental decisions not to have their offspring baptized at birth. This has happened in the French Reformed Church, in the Church of Geneva and in the Presbyterian Church (USA).

It can only strengthen the momentum of baptismal renewal thus sketched in outline if we look more closely at what the long reign of infant baptism has done to baptism. My answers are very largely on the debit side of the ledger. I suspect that the creditable achievements of infant baptism's long reign relate not to baptism itself but to other realities, such as the religious unity of the community, which it has fostered.

1. *The domination of infant baptism has cramped historical enquiry*. The shape of the argument whether or not infants were baptized in the earliest centuries has tended to be determined by assumptions drawn from later experience when infant baptism prevailed unchallenged: infants either were, or were not, baptized, that is, all infants, for the era of Christendom provided no example of mixed practice. Hence historical possibilities were excluded, such as the baptism not of all infants but, to start with at least, only of dying infants. A plausible case can be made for a normal practice of baptizing the newborn having developed by the regularizing of clinical paedobaptism.[7] Other historical possibilities excluded by Christendom assumptions include regional variations, major fluctuations over time (the fourth century witnessed a long-lasting eclipse of infant baptism) and some diversity of practice in actual fact, without any principled undergirding. My generation grew up knowing only 'baptist' churches and paedobaptist churches; surely it had always been so.

---

[7] Cf. D.F. Wright, 'The Origins of Infant Baptism – Child Believers' Baptism?', *Scottish Journal of Theology* 40 (1987), 1–23.

2. *Christendom's regnant paedobaptism fostered exaggerated historical claims, especially about the New Testament era and the next centuries.* Against sixteenth-century Anabaptists, later Baptists and the twentieth century's Karl Barth, it mattered immensely that baby baptism could be shown to be apostolic. Christendom's millennium-and-a-half dependence on infant baptism alone created a massive presumption in favour of its originality. The middle decades of the last century saw some historically inflated studies dedicated to demonstrating just that. As an undergraduate I remember Professor C.F.D. (Charlie) Moule commenting on the book *Infant Baptism in the First Four Centuries* by Joachim Jeremias to the effect that 'It contained at least all the evidence.'[8] Oscar Cullmann was another maximalist,[9] but perhaps the greatest of all was Professor T.F. Torrance of New College, University of Edinburgh. He chaired the Church of Scotland's Special Commission on Baptism during 1953–63, producing most of its voluminous reports in what must rank as the most comprehensive investigation of baptism ever undertaken in the history of the Christian church. It was theologically rather than historically driven and in particular read too much into the early patristic texts.[10] The pervasiveness of its Christendom assumptions became overt when the Church of Scotland's legislative Act anent Baptism in 1963 made no provision for other than infant baptism.

---

[8] Joachim Jeremias, *Infant Baptism in the First Four Centuries* (trans. David Cairns; London: SCM Press, 1960); German original published in 1958.

[9] Oscar Cullmann, *Baptism in the New Testament* (trans. J.K.S. Reid; Studies in Biblical Theology 1; London: SCM Press, 1950); published in German in 1948.

[10] For details see Nigel M. de S. Cameron, David F. Wright et al. (eds.), *Dictionary of Scottish Church History and Theology* (Edinburgh: T&T Clark, 1993), 57–58. The Commission and its reception deserve further study.

3. *Infant baptism took over and monopolized the theology of baptism.* This is inescapable in the work of the Special Commission in Scotland. If baptism as administered was and had been always, or almost always, infant baptism, then the former came to be interpreted largely or wholly in terms of the latter. This was part of the legacy of the Reformers as theological writers and of the formularies of the Reformation churches. The first two *Book(s) of Common Prayer* of Edward VI, issued in 1549 and 1552, had no service for 'The Ministration of Baptism to Such as are of Riper Years', which was the title of the service compiled late in the day in 1661 and included in the 1662 *Book*. The Preface to the 1662 *Book*, explaining this addition, says that it was

> not so necessary when the former Book [1552/59] was compiled, yet by the growth of Anabaptism, through the licentiousness of the late times crept in amongst us, is now become necessary, and may be always useful for the baptizing of natives in our plantations, and others converted to the faith.

The first Scottish *Book of Common Order* of 1564, often known as Knox's Liturgy, showed no awareness of a need for other than infant baptism. Several of the continental Reformers entertained early doubts about the propriety of baptizing babies, and some, including Luther and Calvin, in their first writings on baptism, directed against erroneous Catholic teaching, stressed the necessity of faith for profitable reception, in terms that might even have suggested they were believers-baptists. But the emergence of the Anabaptists' protests posed a much graver challenge, and turned them all into the most uncompromising apologists for paedobaptism. This shift is easily recognizable in Luther by comparing his *Defence of All the Articles*

Condemned by the Recent Bull of Leo X of 1520 with his *Concerning Rebaptism* of 1528, and in Calvin by comparing within the final edition of his *Institutes* Book 4:15, most of which derives from the 1536 edition, with Book 4:16 from the 1539 expansion.

It was in this context that arguments were advanced for the first time in favour of baby baptism as a superior – safer or more evangelical – form of baptism than faith baptism. This had not happened before because the Anabaptists were the first to raise a substantive and sustained opposition to baptizing infants. In order to declare the baptism of a non-speaking baby much more secure, Luther seized on the fickleness of human faith, which might one day request and receive baptism and the next day decide it had not really believed and so seek baptism again. Only the long reign of infant baptism could have allowed the passivity of the baby who has to be carried to baptism to become an illustration of the priority of grace over faith, of divine initiative over any human response. It might serve as an attractive homiletic touch in relation to the baptism of helpless babies, but it is grossly misleading if asserted of Christian baptism as a whole. Even more lamentable (I choose the word advisedly) is that appeal to the wailing of unhappy babies at the font as evidence of God's grace overcoming recalcitrant human resistance. This fancy goes back to no less than Augustine.[11] I am relieved to report that although he abused the words of Jesus in the Gospel parable, 'Go out into the roads and lanes and compel

---

[11] See my essay, 'Augustine and the Transformation of Baptism', in Alan Kreider (ed.), *The Origins of Christendom in the West* (Edinburgh, New York: T&T Clark, 2001), 287–310, at 297–98. Cramer, *Baptism and Change*, 3, has commented: 'Indeed, the child, and the small body of the child with its vulnerable nakedness and its suggestions of uncertainties and precariousness, perhaps replaced water as the central symbol of baptism.'

Infant Baptism in the Hands of Christendom

people to come in' (Lk. 14:23, NRSV), Augustine did not advocate coercing reluctant adult pagans to be plunged into the baptistery kicking and screaming.

Listen to this seductively impressive statement of this kind of theologizing, from the popular English Congregationalist, Bernard Lord Manning (1892–1941):

> In baptism the main thing is not what men do, but what God has done. It is a sign that Christ claims all men as His own and that He has redeemed them to a new way of life. That is why we baptise children ... The water of baptism declares that they are already entitled to all God's mercies to men in the passion of Christ. Your own baptism ought then to mean much to you. It ought to mean all the more because it happened before you knew, or could know, anything about it. Christ redeemed you on the first Good Friday without any thought or action on your part. It is right therefore that as He acted in the first instance, without waiting for any sign of faith from you, so Baptism, the sign of the benefits of His Kingdom, should come to you without waiting for any faith or desire on your part. Every time we baptise a child, we declare to the whole world in the most solemn manner that God does for us what He does without our merits and even without our knowledge. In baptism, more plainly perhaps than anywhere else, God commends His love toward us that *while we were yet sinners* Christ died for us.[12]

Mannings's words are quoted by an English Methodist theologian who acknowledges that not all of the New Testament's presentations of baptism can be applied to the

---

[12] Bernard Lord Manning, *Why Not Abandon the Church?* (London: Independent Press, 1939), 47–48; the italics are his. The last three sentences, perhaps via Flemington (see next note), became part of the preamble to infant baptism used by the Rev James Philip in his long ministry in Holyrood Abbey Church of Scotland, Edinburgh.

case of infants.[13] We then end up with two theologies at best, or at worst with what is applicable to infants squeezing out the rest.

Less objectionable is the following declaration which, from its origin in the French Reformed Church, has found its way into the most recent Church of Scotland *Book of Common Order* and other service books:

> N ...,
> for you Jesus Christ came into the world:
> for you he lived and showed God's love;
> for you he suffered the darkness of Calvary
> and cried at the last, 'It is accomplished';
> for you he triumphed over death
> and rose in newness of life;
> for you he ascended to reign at God's right hand.
> All this he did for you, N ...,
> though you do not know it yet.
> and so the word of Scripture is fulfilled:
> 'We love because God loved us first.'[14]

This is fine until we come to the last two lines and the quotation of 1 John 4:19. The citation of 'We love' in this context is premature, and indeed the verse in its original setting suggests a response to God's known prior love of us.

---

[13] W.F. Flemington, *The New Testament Doctrine of Baptism* (London: SPCK, 1957), 137. Flemington omitted, 'We do not baptise [children] because we or they have faith. That is sloppy Nonconformist sentimentalism. We do not baptise them in order to make them children of God. That is the false and hideous doctrine of Romanists and Anglo-Catholics. We baptise children because they are already God's. They are not outside His Kingdom until it occurs to them to enter it or until it occurs to us to push them into it.'

[14] *Book of Common Order of the Church of Scotland* (Edinburgh: St Andrew Press, 1994), 89.

We will shortly seek to demonstrate how the universal prevalence of infant baptism has had the effect of placing too much of the New Testament's witness to baptism off-limits, as it were, as though inapplicable to infant subjects of the sacrament. Union with Christ has rarely been to the fore, unlike regeneration. The New Testament's wide range of imagery depicting baptismal transition or transformation has likewise been at a discount. In the modern era, infant baptism seems often to have attracted to itself more affective, even sentimental theological notes than soteriological ones.

4. *The Reformation's perpetuation of infant baptism alongside its insistence on 'faith alone' in time contributed to a reductionist view of baptism.* Churches which issued directly or later indirectly from the Reformation maintained an emphasis not only on *sola Scriptura*, 'Scripture alone' – to which the Anabaptists claimed to be more faithful than the mainstream Reformers – but also on 'faith alone'. This would in due course foster a baptismal reductionism as the weight-bearing focus shifted from infant baptism to a later profession of faith, in admission to communicant membership or confirmation. During my student years this was certainly the attitude of much of evangelical Anglicanism, and it remains so among significant areas of the Church of Scotland. I have known of occasions when, of a group of candidates for admission to communion on profession of faith, the one who had not been baptized received baptism not in the main service but shortly beforehand in the presence of the elders alone. Such a practice places a rite of the church's devising above the ordinance of Christ. But it is at least understandable. Numerous ministers cannot in all conscience affirm of infant baptism most of the New Testament's baptismal passages, and until recently their churches' service books have not helped them to do so. The

Church of England's *Book of Common Prayer* from 1549 onwards used Jesus' blessing of the children in Mark 10:13–16 but no explicitly baptismal passage, and the same was true of other denominational baptismal orders of service. Only recently has that Markan incident (or its parallel in Matthew or Luke) been removed from infant-baptism services as central place is at last given to baptismal texts proper.

The Reformers' own convictions about infant baptism, if one may generalize about different trajectories within Reformation teaching, were considerably more full-blooded than many later generations of evangelical churchmen have been able to stomach. They held in the main to realist, rather than merely symbolical, beliefs about what God effected through baptism. I have argued elsewhere that the divines who laboured so long and hard on the Westminster Assembly's benches clearly held to regeneration as God's normal baptismal gift.[15] The erosion of such full-bodied teaching about infant baptism among Protestant evangelicals in modern times distances them from the Reformers more markedly than on almost any other topic. The process has been promoted by the pressure to come to terms – serious conscientious terms – with baptism given so widely to infants and so infrequently leading to active discipleship. If baptism administered indiscriminately to babies on request proves so ineffectual, it cannot retain much doctrinal significance. The logic is

---

[15] Cf. David F. Wright, 'Baptism at the Westminster Assembly', in John H. Leith (ed.), *The Westminster Confession in Current Thought* (Calvin Studies VIII; Davidson College, NC, 1996), 76–90; reprinted in J. Ligon Duncan (ed.), *The Westminster Confession into the 21st Century*, Vol. 1 (Fearn, Ross-shire: Christian Focus Publications, 2003), 161–85. It is also worth pointing out that the Westminster Confession of Faith's statement on baptism moves from baptism on profession of faith to infant baptism (28:4), as earlier had done the Second Helvetic Confession (20); cf. Leith (ed.), *Creeds*, 224, 169.

simple and unchallengeable, and it has a further extension. If paedobaptism counts for so little, carries so little clout, why bother resisting, often at some emotional cost, requests for it from parents who show next to no sign of genuine commitment to it? Anglican evangelicals not so long ago had a habit of talking about such baptismal occasions as 'good boats to fish from', that is, welcome evangelistic opportunities. Such is the colour of a baptismally-reductionist church culture.

5. *The Augustinian theology which paved the way for the universalizing of infant baptism in the early medieval West itself had consequences detrimental to baptism.* That theology centred in the original sin, both guilt and incapacity, inherited by all the sons and daughters of Adam. It necessitated baptism if one was to escape condemnation to hell for the guilt of original sin, irrespective of whether one had lived long enough to add sins of one's own. I remember Peter Brown, a distinguished biographer of Augustine and brilliant interpreter of religion in late antiquity, showing a small postgraduate class in Oxford an illustration in an early printing of Augustine's anti-Pelagian works. It depicted two mothers carrying their babies to the church for baptism. One arrived safely and was baptized, the other died on the way. It said it all.

Given perinatal and infant mortality rates for centuries to come, such a theology of baptism dictated its administration promptly after birth and often in an emergency. This found expression in a common rubric prescribing that the newborn be baptized *quam primum*, 'as soon as possible', which remained in force until after the Second Vatican Council.[16] Inevitably many baptisms took place in private, with the minimum of ceremonial, often with the mother

---

[16] Cf. Maxwell E. Johnson, *The Rites of Christian Initiation: Their Evolution and Interpretation* (Collegeville, MN: Liturgical Press, 1999), 213–15, and for the recent change, 319–21.

still recovering from the birth and not present, and, most critically, without waiting for a priest to be summoned. So baptism – in practice, of course, almost invariably baby baptism – had to be capable of being validly administered by laypeople, even heretics or schismatics and even themselves unbaptized.[17] Augustine had provided the theological rationale, but he could not have foreseen the extent to which laymen or much more often laywomen close to the mother at delivery took over the priestly function, with the concomitant diminution of baptism itself in its ecclesial dimensions. The Augustinian key was that the true minister of the sacraments was Christ, so that its validity and efficacy were not dependent on the personal standing of the human agent. All that mattered was that water and the Trinitarian formula were used.[18]

A moment's thought reveals how badly baby baptism of this sort suffered by comparison with the eucharist. By the later Middle Ages the Catholic Church had recognized other sacraments besides the two dominical institutions which alone the Reformation would accept. The Catholic insistence, spelt out at the Fourth Lateran Council in 1215 against Waldensian and other heretics, that the eucharistic transubstantiation could be effected only by a priest ordained according to the apostolic succession, contrasts starkly with the freedom countenanced in the ministering of baptism. It has been said that most of the babies baptized in the later medieval West were baptized by

---

[17] Cf. Thomas Aquinas, *Summa Theologiae* IIIa.67.5. Although Augustine left the issue unresolved, 'It has subsequently been determined by the Church that unbaptized persons, whether Jews or pagans, can confer the sacrament of baptism, so long as they baptize in the Church's manner (*in forma Ecclesiae*).'

[18] David F. Wright, 'Donatist Theologoumena in Augustine? Baptism, Reviviscence of Sins and Unworthy Ministers', in *Congresso Internazionale su S. Agostino … Atti II* (Rome: Institutum Patristicum Augustinianum, 1987), 213 – 24.

midwives. This is almost certainly an exaggeration, but midwives were baptizing with sufficient frequency for handbooks to contain sections dealing with their baptismal role and for midwives' religious allegiance to be a matter for ecclesiastical concern.[19]

The rite of baptism in the *Sarum Manual*, a service book widely used in England in the late medieval era (*Sarum* is Latin for 'Salisbury'), has a lengthy appendix which tells parish priests frequently on Sunday to

> explain to ... parishioners the form of baptizing in pure, natural and fresh water, and in no other liquid, so that if necessity arise they may know how to baptize infants according to the form of the Church, using the form of words of baptism ... without any addition, subtraction, interpretation, alteration, corruption or transposition.[20]

The appendix continues with instructions on what should happen if a child thus baptized in an emergency survives to be brought to the church. Careful enquiry is made whether the layperson did the baptism correctly or not. In any case of doubt the priest must conditionally rebaptize ('if thou art baptized I do not rebaptize thee; but if thou art not yet baptized, I baptize thee ...'), and in every case the priest administers all the other elements of the rite apart from the essential kernel.[21] It is also laid down that if both a man and a woman are present when a baby urgently needs baptism, the man is to baptize, 'unless the woman happened to know well the sacramental words'.[22]

---

[19] Cf. David Cressy, *Birth, Marriage, and Death. Ritual, Religion, and the Life-Cycle in Tudor and Stuart England* (Oxford: Oxford University Press, 1997), 117–23.
[20] J.D.C. Fisher, *Christian Initiation: Baptism in the Medieval West* (Alcuin Club Collections 47; London: SPCK, 1965), 175.
[21] Ibid., 176.
[22] Ibid., 177.

6. *The hold of infant baptism has been so strong for so long in Western Christianity that, since the re-emergence of the case for believers' baptism (first seriously in the sixteenth century with the Anabaptists), it has tended to be reactive and inadequate.* Let me advance the bold and surely overstated assertion that it has consequently proved difficult for Baptist churches to develop strong theologies of baptism. I remain surprised at the laxity of too many Baptist churches, including some which should know and do better, in relating baptism to church membership, and office-holding, quite apart from the 'testimony' culture which still dominates too many Baptist services of baptism. Without doubt the perceived weakness of much Baptist understanding of baptism has hindered or delayed its becoming central in ecumenical dialogues. The Baptists were simply not taken seriously enough, even in respect of their raison d'être (to judge by their name), the doctrine of baptism itself.

The causes of this situation must be many and varied, and its remedy has been often attempted and probably in recent decades with greater vigour and sophistication than ever before.[23] The point I am making, that paradoxically the insufficiency of much Baptist baptismal thinking owes something to its being reactive against an unhealthily

---

[23] Cf. the important symposium edited by Anthony R. Cross and Philip E. Thompson, *Baptist Sacramentalism* (Studies in Baptist History and Thought 5; Carlisle: Paternoster Press, 2003). Much popular and not-so-popular Baptist understanding of baptism has insisted on faith preceding baptism – and often allowed it to do so by an indefinite interval – over against the paedobaptist defence of baptism preceding faith, sometimes expressed as the priority of grace over faith. The pervasive testimony-to-my-experience-of-Christ ethos of Baptist baptism sometimes seems like a grossly exaggerated reaction against the baptism of non-confessing babies. Cf. also Lennart Johnsson, *Baptist Reconsideration of Baptism and Ecclesiology* (European University Studies XXIII: 716; Frankfurt am Main: Peter Lang, 2000), on Sweden, and Anthony R. Cross, *Baptism and the Baptists. Theology and Practice in Twentieth-Century Britain* (Carlisle: Paternoster Press, 2000).

regnant infant baptism, would require careful scholarly demonstration to be wholly convincing. But the thesis should not strike us as too unbelievable, if we recall the circumstances in which the first modern Baptists, the Anabaptists, made their stand and came to the fore. They opposed much more in the magisterial Reformations than infant baptism, including fundamentally the church-state alliance and the use of the coercive powers of state authorities in defence of the new Protestantism. Infant baptism belonged to the complex that I have called 'Christendom', which survived, albeit much transformed, the turmoil of the Reformation. Rejection of paedobaptism not only set the Radicals against both the Old Church and the new evangelical churches but also put in jeopardy their belonging to the civil community, coterminous as it was with the infant-baptized church of the city or the region. Religious dissent had inseparable social and political implications, and the Anabaptists suffered repression in many places. They interpreted their persecutions as a baptism of blood in which they were identified with the sufferings of Christ. Their afflictions were a further confirmation, a further seal, of their being members of Christ's body.[24]

This appropriation of the theme of Christ's death was, however, no substitute for their poor grasp of the objectivity of baptism as itself dying and rising with Christ. They seem to have been reluctant to discern in water baptism, which they mostly distinguished from a prior baptism of the Spirit, a decisive action of God himself. Concluding his examination of four highly prominent Anabaptist writers on baptism, R.S. Armour summarizes as follows:

---

[24] Cf. Rollin Stely Armour, *Anabaptist Baptism: A Representative Study* (Studies in Anabaptist and Mennonite History 11; Scottdale, PA: Herald Press, 1966), 141.

[T]hey were at one in saying that the only legitimate basis for receiving baptism and entering the baptismal covenant was the experience of regeneration within, a regeneration which gave the believer power to make a valid confession of faith and to keep the commands of Christ under the watchful eye of a disciplining church.[25]

Thus baptism was to be given 'only to those in whom the gifts of rebirth were evident'.[26] The objective force of baptism was to be found in the church's witness answering to the candidate's confession:

Thus, the baptizand not only *gave* a testimony as he witnessed to his faith through the sign of baptism, but he *received* a testimony – specifically, he received from the church the sign of their belief that they recognized the gift of the Spirit within him.[27]

Although the worldwide Baptist churches of later centuries do not stand in direct historical continuity with these sixteenth-century pioneers, it is not difficult to discern in Armour's summary an approach to baptism not unfamiliar among Baptists today. Is it far-fetched to identify here a rebound rejection of any notion of baptism as itself an act of divine grace? They had hoped that the early Reformers' protests against Catholicism's automatic (*ex opere operato*) sacramental efficacy by playing up the necessity of faith might have led on to a more rigorous Biblicism. Instead, once the Anabaptist voice was raised, the Reformers resiled from their original stress on faith as absolutely essential for fruitful baptism into a defence of infant baptism which Radicals branded as another symptom of the

---

[25] Ibid., 135.
[26] Ibid., 138.
[27] Ibid., 140, italics his.

new Catholicism or the new papalism of mainline Protestants relying on the state.

Recent trends in ecumenical reflection on baptism must be regarded as favourable to Baptists' fundamental demand for baptism on profession of faith. Believers Baptists now have an unprecedented opportunity to promote a theology of baptism which confidently takes the full measure of the New Testament witness and no longer feeds on reaction against the distorting effects of the long reign of infant baptism.

7. *The New Testament's presentation of baptism became remote, and baptism could no longer function as a key to the character of the church.* This further consequence of the unchallenged dominance of baby baptism has been touched on more than once in this lecture but merits fuller attention. It is true that New Testament baptism was conversion baptism in a context of primary mission, rather than baptism administered in maintenance of a well-founded church in a Christian country. But if we overstate the historical distinctiveness of early Christian practice, we end up having little or nothing to say for the church today about baptism from the New Testament. As Oscar Cullmann used to argue, the apostolic church does indeed belong to the once-for-all nature of the mission of Christ himself, but that strengthens, not dissolves, its normative character for all subsequent churches.[28]

Baptism is invoked as a reference point in the apostolic writings often enough to sustain the claim that the church is a baptismal community – more obviously so in New Testament terms than it is a eucharistic community, as is so often asserted of it. It is a mark of the church's unity, according to Ephesians 4:5, 'one Lord, one faith, one baptism' (and note the absence of 'one Lord's supper'). Hence

---

[28] See Cullmann's essay, 'The Tradition', in his *The Early Church* (trans. and ed. A.J.B. Higgins; London: SCM Press, 1956), 55–99.

in trying to defuse divisiveness among Corinth's Christians Paul could challenge those who distinguished themselves as followers of him with the words, 'Was Paul crucified for you? Were you baptised into the name of Paul?' (1 Cor. 1:13). Baptism was a unifying focus also in the sense that it was a great leveller:

> You are all sons of God through faith in Christ Jesus, for all of you who were baptised into Christ have clothed yourselves with Christ. There is neither Jew nor Greek, slave nor free, male nor female, for you are all one in Christ Jesus.
> (Gal. 3:26–28)

The Keswick Convention's great motto, 'All One in Christ Jesus', is in origin a baptismal affirmation. Scholars deduce that the baptismal rite must have included a declaration 'There is neither Jew nor Greek, slave nor free', etc., perhaps as an invitation to all to come forward, since the two parallels to Galatians 3 are also baptismal. We all 'form one body,' says Paul, 'For we were all baptised by one Spirit into one body – whether Jews or Greeks, slave or free' (1 Cor. 12:12–13). Similarly, when Paul writes to the Colossians, 'Here there is no Greek or Jew, circumcised or uncircumcised, barbarian, Scythian, slave or free' (Col. 3:11), it follows his reminder that they have divested themselves of the old self and put on the new, which is most likely baptismal imagery.

At this point it is worth asking ourselves how instinctively we address issues of disunity and unity by appealing to the implications of our common baptism. It is certainly a way of proceeding which infant baptism has rendered hugely more implausible. It is something of a commonplace nowadays to talk about baptism as the ordination of the laity, the action in which all Christians are commissioned for witness and service. Again it is difficult to make that meaningful in an infant-baptizing community. If our infant baptism was ordination, it was totally different in every respect from the ordination of particular individuals with which we are familiar. Such theology suffers from a profound sense of unreality.

Paul's preaching of the free grace of the gospel was so convincing that some concluded, 'Let's go on sinning so that grace may go on increasing' (cf. Rom. 6:1). How did Paul correct this disturbing misapprehension?

> Don't you know that all of us who were baptised into Christ Jesus were baptised into his death? We were therefore buried with him through baptism into death in order that, just as Christ was raised from the dead through the glory of the Father, we too may live a new life.
> (Rom. 6:3–4)

Again the question is obvious: how many of us would have contemplated countering that misunderstanding by exposing the meaning of baptism? Here we meet another illustration of the way baptism functioned as a criterion, a touchstone of authentic Christianity. It rarely does so, I suggest, in contemporary experience, even in Baptist circles. That we have largely lost the self-consciousness of being a baptismal community owes something to the remoteness of New Testament baptism induced by a dominant, and often devalued, paedobaptism.

Hence a major recovery programme is called for. There can be no better starting-point, and for evangelicals no other starting-point, than a re-appropriation of the New Testament witness to early Christian baptism. I strongly recommend such Bible study to infant baptizers and believer baptizers alike.

2

Baptism and Profession of Faith
What? Whose?

'Believers' baptism' has always seemed a preferable usage to 'adult baptism', which is something else we should debit to the account of predominant infant baptism. 'Infant' in its own way is also misleading when one considers the age span it commonly denotes in contemporary English, as in infants' school. 'Baby baptism' is more accurate but strikes some participants in the debate as prejudicial because it seems disrespectful, even flippant. 'Infant baptism' still retains a certain gravity, and, for those who take Latin etymology seriously, is precisely the right phrase, since 'infant' derives from a Latin compound *infans*, meaning 'not speaking, not yet able to speak'. That, as we shall see, not age, is the decisive criterion. The combination of 'infant' and 'adult' leaves a large lacuna occupied by young teenagers and others. The 1662 *Book of Common Prayer* service for the baptism of 'Such as Are of Riper Years, and Able to Answer for Themselves' still provides for their nomination in advance by parents or 'other discreet persons' and for their accompaniment by godfathers and godmothers. How common in the history of the church has been child believers' baptism awaits, to my knowledge, thorough investigation. Perhaps a Southern Baptist historian has already traced the antecedents of that communion's practice.

'[B]aptism upon personal profession of faith is the most clearly attested pattern in the New Testament documents', as *Baptism, Eucharist and Ministry* put it in 1982.[1] They portray no tidy consistency of procedure, but the intimate association between being a believer and being baptized is inescapable, both in that faith and its profession are a requirement for baptism and also, let us note, in that having become a believer necessitates baptism to seal, as it were, that status. When Lydia and her household had been baptized at Philippi, she invited Paul and company to her home with the words, 'If you consider me a believer in the Lord, come and stay at my house' (Acts 16:15). The Philippian jailer responded to Paul's instruction, 'Believe in the Lord Jesus and you will be saved' by being immediately baptized – the text does not mention his believing – and then 'he was filled with joy because he had come to believe in God' (Acts 16:31–34). If infants were included in these household baptisms, they were so as believers.

Early Christianity, and here we move beyond the New Testament into the next four centuries, knew nothing of an unbaptized believer. Augustine later discussed more than once whether a catechumen, a person being prepared for baptism, should be called a 'Christian'. He concludes not without hesitation that he may – but by virtue, so to speak, of his forthcoming baptism.[2] Just as the church itself could be described as a baptismal community, so baptism was essential to the identity of the individual Christian. The Greek word πιστός and the Latin *fidelis*, both strictly meaning 'believers', came to denote a baptized person in the

---

[1] *Baptism, Eucharist and Ministry*. 4.

[2] Cf. Cornelius Mayer (ed.), *Augustinus-Lexikon*, Vol. 1 (Basel: Schwabe & Co. AG, 1986–94), 788–94, s.v. 'Catechumenus' (Emilien Lamirande) at 789, for references and literature. Elsewhere Augustine often seemed to restrict 'Christian' to the baptized, to which category *fidelis*, 'believer', was certainly restricted.

church of the Fathers. In numerous epitaph inscriptions of children extant from around the Mediterranean, one of those two words designated the child who had died as baptized, often with the date given. They include cases of very young babies clearly incapable of being commemorated as 'believers' in a literal sense.[3]

This was a very different world – and church – from what most of us are familiar with today. That we find ourselves where we now are, with, for example, the label 'Christian' applied in evangelical circles to converted believers irrespective of baptism but certainly not to baptized infants, is, I believe, inexplicable without the pervasive effects of baptismal reductionism wrought by the hegemony of paedobaptism in Christendom, although it can hardly furnish the whole explanation. If I have one overarching aim in these lectures, it is to foster an enhanced appreciation of baptism among Christians and their churches, particularly within the evangelical constituency.

If we ask what it was that baptizands professed in their baptism, the New Testament and the first post-apostolic writings give no precise picture. Nevertheless, we may be sure that they orally declared their faith in Jesus Christ as Lord and Saviour or Son of God or some other title or combination of titles. There can have been no single prescribed formula, and in Gentile contexts it may have been from the outset necessary to include also faith in the one God, Creator and Father of Christ the Son. Scholars have devoted much productive attention to the development in the New Testament and beyond of formulae of lesser or greater

---

[3] Cf. E. Ferguson, 'Inscriptions and the Origins of Infant Baptism', *Journal of Theological Studies* 30 (1979), 37–46; reprinted in Ferguson (ed.), *Studies in Early Christianity* (18 Vols; New York: Garland Publishing, 1993), Vol. 11: *Conversion, Catechumenate and Baptism in the Early Church*, 391–400.

length and fixity of wording expressing central Christian beliefs.[4] These beginnings of the first Christian confessions or creeds were located in several different settings in early Christianity. One such might have been worship, another witness in front of hostile Roman officials, but without doubt the most creative context was baptism. It would not be too much to say that baptism was the wellspring of the church's first creeds. They developed in response to demands that would have varied from place to place, although the imperative to exclude heretical teachings must have been felt almost everywhere. Yet what happened at Rome tended to be influential elsewhere, which brings us to a highly important text calling for extended consideration. It has had a massive impact on studies of early Christian church order and worship for the last half-century and more, and almost as big an impact on modern liturgical revision. Its influence behind texts such as *Baptism, Eucharist and Ministry* has been profound, and we now, since 2002, have the advantage of a first-rate commentary on it in English.

This work is known as the *Apostolic Tradition* and traditionally ascribed to Hippolytus, who flourished at Rome in the early decades of the third century. Almost everything concerning this text remains the subject of lively scholarly argument, and Hippolytus's identity is difficult to establish with confidence, since he may have been more than one person. The opinion of Paul Bradshaw and his colleagues, authors of the first commentary, denies its attribution to Hippolytus and judges the work to be

---

[4] For helpful surveys see Gerald F. Hawthorne and Ralph P. Martin (eds.), *Dictionary of Paul and his Letters* (Downers Grove, IL/Leicester: InterVarsity Press, 1993), 190–92 (Martin), and Ralph P. Martin and Peter H. Davids (eds.), *Dictionary of the Later New Testament & Its Developments* (Downers Grove, IL/Leicester: InterVarsity Press, 1997), 255–60 (D.F. Wright).

an aggregation of material from different sources, quite possibly arising from different geographical regions and probably from different historical periods, from perhaps as early as the mid-second century to as late as the mid-fourth, since none of the textual witnesses to it can be dated with any certainty before the last quarter of that century.[5]

Such a multilayered compilation and its claim to convey 'apostolic tradition' are typical of church order documents, that is, manuals which set out how churches should order their activities, in baptizing, holding the Lord's supper, ordaining, praying, fasting and much more besides. The work's account of the complex baptismal ceremony and preparations for it is of absolutely capital importance, and most of it is attributed by Bradshaw and his fellow authors to a core document dating from perhaps the middle of the second century.[6] The *Apostolic Tradition* (as it will surely continue to be conventionally called) will concern us in the next lecture also. Here we confine ourselves to profession of faith.

The instruction for baptism places 'the little children' first, with a distinction between those who can speak for themselves, who shall indeed do so, and those who cannot, for whom parents or other family members will speak. Then the men are to be baptized and finally the women.[7] The traditional date of the *Apostolic Tradition*, ca. 220, made this almost the earliest unambiguous reference to infant

---

[5] Paul F. Bradshaw, Maxwell E. Johnson and L. Edward Phillips, *The Apostolic Tradition. A Commentary* (Hermeneia; Minneapolis, MN: Fortress Press, 2002), 14. A simplified text in English is available in Geoffrey J. Cuming, *Hippolytus: A Text for Students* (Grove Liturgical Study 8; Bramcote, Notts: Grove Books, 1976).

[6] Bradshaw et al., *Apostolic Tradition*, 14–15.

[7] Hippolytus, *Apostolic Tradition* 21:4–5, Bradshaw et al., *Apostolic Tradition*, 112–13.

baptism. On the new edition's dating of the core document in the text to the mid-second century, it would be the earliest by some decades. It also attests the routine baptizing of infants, and on either dating it is the earliest record of this kind. We notice immediately the differentiation, within the children, it seems, between those who can and those who cannot answer for themselves. This is the first such precise differentiation among candidates for baptism in Christian history, but it leaves fascinating questions unanswered. Is a child's physical and mental capacity in view, or is the ability more juridical, implying the Roman recognition that at the age of seven children entered into certain rights to speak for themselves? Augustine and Jerome would later treat seven as a new age of Christian responsibility, Augustine in connexion with the baptism of a boy speaking for himself. In what terms a parent or other relative spoke for a non-responding child we do not know, and no source tells us until ca. 400. This is in fact the only reference to young children in the long baptismal service in the *Apostolic Tradition*. The baptism proper was followed immediately by the baptized's first communion, and nothing in the text indicates that the children were not included in it.

The baptism consisted of three immersions, with each candidate answering 'I believe' to the three credal questions.[8] If these three questions were turned into a declarative form and joined together, the result would be recognizable as quite close to the (later) Apostles' Creed. The first question was probably short and very similar to 'Do you believe in God the Father Almighty?' The second was much longer, in words near to the following:

---

[8] Hippolytus, *Apostolic Tradition*, 21:12–18; Bradshaw et al., *Apostolic Tradition*, 114–19.

Do you believe in Jesus Christ, the Son of God who was born by the Holy Spirit from the Virgin Mary and crucified under Pontius Pilate, and died and was buried and rose on the third day alive from the dead and sits on the right hand of the Father, and will come to judge the living and the dead?

The third question was again brief: 'Do you believe in the Holy Spirit and the holy church and the resurrection of the flesh?'

So the churches' first creeds were baptismal and interrogatory in form, as evidence from elsewhere than Rome confirms. Bradshaw and colleagues place this section of material in the mid-second-century core source of the *Apostolic Tradition*. What emerges indisputably from all the records we have is that early Christian services of baptism were constructed for responding believers, with little children accommodated by others providing what the service demanded and what the children could not themselves supply. There is no trace of a service designed specifically for infants. Also worth stressing is that the faith professed was the faith of the church which the candidate made his or her own. The baptizands did not make up their own testimony or speak about their own experience. The point is germane to what may have been said on behalf of the non-speaking youngsters. It must have corresponded in some way to what the responding candidates professed. It cannot in the nature of the case have had anything to do with their own religious history, of which they had none.

It is not until the early years of the fifth century, in Augustine in the Latin West and Asterius in the Greek East, that we encounter the first evidence of how parents or others did speak for the children. (This Asterius is known solely as the author of some thirty-odd homilies on the early Psalms. He was earlier wrongly identified with two other individuals of the same name and consequently dated in the early fourth century.[9]) In the context of the credal questions the parent was asked in respect of a child, 'Does he/she believe?', to which the reply was 'He/She believes.' Question and answer were given in the third person, however remarkable that may seem to us.[10] Whatever else might be said about this disclosure, it confirms beyond peradventure that baptism in the early church was constructed as a rite for faith-professing participants, and that infants took part as believers whose belief, whatever that might mean, was expressed by others.

This account of things may surprise you, if you have assimilated what appears like a decidedly divergent story of early baptismal development – that, whether or not the baptizing of the newborn began in the apostolic era, it subsequently became, by, say, the third century, the common practice. What I have presented about the baptismal liturgy does not in fact conflict with that kind of outline history. The question how general paedobaptism in fact was is another issue. If one adopts the reading of the evidence given by Joachim Jeremias in *Infant Baptism in the First Four Centuries* (1958/1960), then one must believe both that in the early fifth century infant baptism was all but universal for the children of Christians – and that all such children were baptized by the procedure attested by Augustine and

---

[9] On Asterius the Homilist see Wolfram Kinzig, *In Search of Asterius. Studies on the Authorship of the Homilies on the Psalms* (Göttingen: Vandenhoeck & Ruprecht, 1990). The use made by Jeremias, *Infant Baptism*, 15, 69, 91, 93, of the evidence of 'Asterius the Sophist' now needs revision.

[10] See J.C. Didier, 'Une adaptation de la liturgie baptismale au baptême des enfants dans l'Église ancienne', *Mélanges de science religieuse* 22 (1965), 79–90; R. De Latte, 'Saint Augustin et le baptême: Étude liturgico-historique du ritual baptismal des enfants chez S. Augustin', *Questions liturgiques* 57 (1976), 41–55. Both authors wrote before the date of Asterius was revised.

Asterius. No alternative means of dealing with those too young to answer for themselves has left any trace.

You may reckon that it is easier to accept this version of baptismal practice if only a small number, a minority, of candidates for baptism were infants, and conversely that it strains credulity if nearly all were infants. In reality, in the years when Augustine and Asterius left us their records, infant baptisms were still very much in the minority, according to my interpretation of the evidence, which differs considerably from that of Jeremias. Now is not the occasion to argue the case, which rests on a great deal of hard evidence in the fourth and early fifth centuries that the offspring of Christian parents – the known offspring of known Christian parents – were not baptized as babies.[11] So the statements of our two witnesses, Augustine and Asterius, may well fit better with my historical construction than with Jeremias's, in terms of infant baptism being at that period very far from majority practice.

Yet the underlying problem is not thereby eased, since the procedure did not change in the Western church once paedobaptism had become all but universal, nor did it change for well over a millennium. To spell it out as simply and starkly as I can, for many centuries when virtually all babies born in Europe were baptized soon after birth, their parents or other sponsors declared in the baptismal ritual that the babies believed. Let us fast forward to the English *Book of Common Prayer* of 1662, which fell out of general use in the Church of England only in the late twentieth century. In the service of 'Publick Baptism of Infants'

---

[11] For a partial treatment of the period, see David F. Wright, 'Infant Dedication in the Early Church', in Stanley E. Porter and Anthony R. Cross (eds.), *Baptism, the New Testament and the Church. Historical and Contemporary Studies in Honour of R.E.O. White* (Journal for the Study of the New Testament, Suppl. Ser. 171; Sheffield: Sheffield Academic Press, 1999), 352–78.

the priest addresses the godfathers and godmothers as follows:

> [T]his infant must also faithfully, for his/her part, promise by you that are his/her sureties, (until he/she come of age to take it upon himself,) that he/she will renounce the devil and all his works, and constantly believe God's holy Word, and obediently keep his commandments.

There follow four questions:

> Dost thou, in the name of this Child, renounce the devil and all his works, etc?
> *Answer*: I renounce them all.
>
> Dost thou believe in God the Father Almighty, Maker of heaven and earth?
> And in Jesus Christ his only-begotten Son our Lord? [the rest of the Apostles' Creed follows]
> *Answer*: All this I steadfastly believe.
>
> Wilt thou be baptized in this faith?
> *Answer*: That is my desire.
>
> Wilt thou then obediently keep God's holy will and commandments, and walk in the same all the days of thy life?
> *Answer*: I will.

How to construe this sequence may be open to subtle explanation. According to the preamble, it is by the godparents that the child promises, but when we come to the questions the text switches into the second person singular 'Dost thou, Wilt thou' and the answers are given in the first person singular. The first phrase of the initial question,

'Dost thou, in the name of this Child', seems an awkward compromise, but, again according to the preamble, we have here the child promising by his or her sureties, not the sureties promising on behalf of the child.

This is the service book of a now, in the mid-seventeenth century, securely reformed church, but this baptismal order is not much of an advance on the one in the earliest prayer book in English in 1549. The sentence in the preamble is almost identical, 'these infants muste also faithfully for theyr parte promise by you, that be theyr suerties' etc., as is the content of the questions. There are eight in number; the Creed takes up three, and in 1662 the first question would combine the first three here in 1549. Yet the rubric prior to the questions and answers is more direct: *'Then shall the priest demaunde of the childe ... these questions following.'*[12] The 1552 *Book*, revised in the light of recommendations from, among others, the eminent continental Reformers then resident in England, Peter Martyr Vermigli and Martin Bucer, changed this rubric to read *'Then shall the priest demaunde of the Godfathers and Godmothers ...'*. It also reduced the questions to three but left their form unchanged.[13] The 1662 *Book* eliminated the rubric, adding instead as the priest's introduction to the questions, 'I demand therefore'. One further difference between 1549 and both of the later books is that in 1549 the priest's first question addresses the child by name. This is absent in 1552 and 1662.

In fact what we find in these prayer books of the Church of England during and after the Reformation is not much different from what obtained in the country prior to the

---

[12] *The First and Second Prayer-Books of King Edward the Sixth* (Everyman's Library; London: J.M. Dent & Sons, New York: E.P. Dutton & Co., n.d.), 239–40.
[13] Ibid., 396–97.

religious upheaval. Probably the most widely used service book in England on the eve of the Reformation was the *Sarum Manual* (*Sarum* being the Latin for 'Salisbury'). This is a standard reference point for historians assessing common liturgical practice just before the changes in the ecclesiastical order. It was in Latin, of course, and the 1549 *Book of Common Prayer* may be viewed as a lightly revised English translation of *Sarum*. *Sarum's* baptism service has the same eight questions as in 1549, with a few differences. An anointing follows the first three renunciation questions, and accordingly the priest names the child at the beginning of the fourth as well as the first question. Several of *Sarum's* questions are briefer than in their first English counterpart, with a noticeably truncated second credal question, 'Dost thou believe also in Jesus Christ his only Son our Lord, who was born and suffered?' Nothing is said in the *Sarum Manual* about the role of the godparents except simply repeatedly 'Let them reply', which they do of course in the first person singular.[14]

We are not here concerned with evaluating how thoroughly the Church of England was reformed in the sixteenth and seventeenth centuries. Indirectly what is exposed by this material is the conservatism that characterizes the forms of words used in the public worship of the church, although that again is not our interest in this lecture. Above all we have observed the remarkable tenacity of a strange feature of the long reign of infant baptism during Christendom. Not far short of a millennium after infant baptism became the more or less universal form of baptism in the West, infants were still being baptized by an awkward adaptation of a rite formulated for the baptism of responding believers – and long after the use of that

---

[14] Fisher, *Christian Initiation: Baptism in the Medieval West*, 172–73.

order of service for persons speaking for themselves had fallen into desuetude. Infant baptism took over from believers' baptism, and in more senses than one, since it apparently lacked the inner power to create its own appropriate liturgical procedures, nor indeed in some theatres of the Reformation could the rediscovery of the biblical gospel provide that dynamic.

It will be important to look at what happened to this aspect of baptism in other Reformation movements than the English, but first, since, as you may have noticed, the lecture jumped from ca. 400 to the sixteenth century, it will be worthwhile to give some selective illustrations of developments in the intervening period. They do but confirm the main lines of the picture painted so far, but given the momentousness of the strange history of infant baptism, there will be value in filling out the story at some points.

At around 500 a deacon in the Church of Rome called John (of whom nothing else is known) answered some questions about baptismal practice put to him by one Senarius. John the Deacon gives a detailed explanation of many aspects of the Roman rite without addressing all of Senarius's questions specifically. Then he adds:

> I must say plainly and at once, in case I seem to have overlooked the point, that all these things are done even to infants, who by reason of their youth understand nothing. And by this you may know that when they are presented by their parents or others, it is necessary that their salvation should come through other people's profession, since their damnation came by another's fault.[15]

---

[15] E.C. Whitaker, *Documents of the Baptismal Liturgy* (3rd edn.; ed. Maxwell E. Johnson; Alcuin Club Collections 79; London: SPCK, 2003), 211.

The rationale he offers for vicarious profession of faith appeared here for neither the first nor the last time, even though its logic is limited, since it was not only babies' damnation that 'came by another's fault', and the New Testament's antitype to Adam is not the Christian but Christ.

What John the Deacon's exposition would mean at Rome in the sixth century may be read in the *Gelasian Sacramentary*, preserved in a manuscript written near Paris in the mid-eighth century but containing the Roman rite of a couple of centuries earlier with some Gallican elements added in. Here we have lengthy liturgical forms of various kinds extending from the preparatory ceremonies during Lent as the fulfilment of the catechumenate right through to the baptism itself at the end of the Easter night vigil and on into the first communion of the baptized. All of this elaborate material had originally been compiled for responding believers as the participants, but all of it is here applied, by rubrical directions with minimal adaptation of content, to infants. Thus the 'opening' of the four Gospels – an account of the meaning of word 'gospel' and of the four symbolic faces of the Evangelists according to Ezekiel 1:10, and a reading of the first section of each Gospel – is solemnly addressed to uncomprehending infants. The Creed is then introduced to 'the elect' (i.e. candidates for Easter baptism), in Greek (an item of information which helps to date the text), and an acolyte reads the Creed to the infants with his hand on the head of one of them, and the priest follows with a medium-length exposition of the Creed. The same procedure obtains for the Lord's Prayer. On the Saturday before Easter Day, the infants, having notionally memorized the Creed since its earlier delivery to them, 'make their return of the Creed', after being catechized and exorcized by the priest and after renouncing Satan and all his works and all his pomps – three questions with the response to each 'I renounce'. The children's rendition of the Creed is effected by the priest's reciting it with his hand on their heads. At the font itself they are asked the three credal questions, the wording of which is close to that of the *Sarum Manual* as printed in 1543, which they each answer – by whose mouth is not indicated – 'I believe'.[16]

The pattern is similar, closely similar, in liturgical manuscript-books from different parts of Europe and different centuries during the Middle Ages. Liturgical experts identify distinctive elements of greater or lesser weight, which enable them to locate and date them and to establish relationships between them. We are not concerned here with such technical detail, since the general picture is common throughout Latin Christendom.

In or near 812, Charlemagne, the supreme sovereign of the new Holy Roman Empire, circulated a letter to his metropolitan bishops enquiring how they and their suffragan bishops taught their priests and the people about baptism, together with detailed questions on constituent aspects of the rite itself.[17] The responses from some of the leading bishops of Europe have recently been edited together for the first time and offer a wonderfully rich tapestry of evidence on baptismal beliefs and practices early in the ninth century. Some of the respondents explained how infants came to be encompassed in a baptismal service requiring a self-conscious profession of faith; Charlemagne had not asked this, although one of his questions mentioned infants.

Theodulf, Bishop of Orleans, recorded that, when children not yet possessed of reason and with little

---

[16] Ibid., 218–25, 229–30.
[17] Susan A. Keefe, *Water and the Word: Baptism and the Education of the Clergy in the Carolingian Empire*, Vol. 2 (2 Vols; Notre Dame, IN: University of Notre Dame Press, 2002), 261–63.

understanding came to an appropriate age, they were taught in the sacraments of the faith and 'the mysteries of their confession'. He deliberately wrote 'their (own) confession' (*suam confessionem*)

> because although they cannot yet speak, those who receive them from the washing of the font both confess and speak for them (*pro illis*). It is rightly fitting that those who are bound by the sins of others should also by the confession of others receive the remission of original sins through the mystery of baptism.[18]

A different approach is taken by Amalarius, archbishop of Trier. Although little children cannot understand conversion and faith,

> we nevertheless believe that they convert to God in the light of the sacrament of conversion, and have faith in the light of the sacrament of faith, as we read in Augustine's letter to bishop Boniface.[19]

This *Letter* 98 of Augustine's is one of our sources for the practice of an infant baptizand's being declared a believer ('He/She believes') by a parent or sponsor.

Boniface had expressed surprise to Augustine that a confident answer could be given by parents or other presenters at that age of the child when he or she does not so much as know that there is a God. Moreover, they would not presume to answer other questions about the child's future character or conduct.[20]

---

[18] Ibid., 292–93. This and the following translations are mine. In a few details they vary from Keefe's punctuation.
[19] Ibid., 348.
[20] Wright, 'Augustine and the Transformation of Baptism', 300. In that essay I followed the general dating of this letter to 408 AD (299–300

Augustine's answer, cited by Amalarius, argues that the sacrament of a reality takes the name of that reality, so that the sacrament of faith comes to be known as faith:

> Therefore a child is made a believer (*fidelem*), though not yet by that faith (*fides*) which resides in the will of those believing, nevertheless already by the sacrament of that faith. For as the reply is given that they believe, so too they are called believers, not by mentally assenting to faith itself but by receiving the sacrament of it.[21]

This was hardly Augustine at his most impressive, but it sufficed for Amalarius. Biblical scholars and theologians of the Carolingian era relied heavily on extensive quotations from the Fathers of the early centuries.

The third reply to Charlemagne's enquiry to be noted here came from Leidrad, Archbishop of Lyons, who devoted a lengthy section of his letter to 'infants, or those who cannot respond for themselves'. It is, to the best of my knowledge, the fullest discussion of the issue encountered so far in the history of Christian baptism:

> The church's custom holds and its recognized teachers (*doctores*) hand down that we celebrate the mysteries of baptism with exactly the same sacramental words for infants as for adults. Hence it is that the priest conducting the sacrament does not question one person on behalf of another, that is, an adult on behalf of the child, whether he renounces the

---

[20] (*Continued*) with n. 35). More recently the early years of the Pelagian controversy, 411–13, have received weighty support from Pierre-Marie Hombert, *Nouvelles recherches de chronologie Augustinienne* (Collection des Études Augustiniennes, Sér. Antiq. 163; Paris: Institut d' Études Augustiniennes, 2000), 161 n. 329.

[21] Keefe, *Water and the Word*, Vol. 2, 349, close to Augustine, *Letter* 98:10.

devil or believes in God, but asks the actual one he is about to baptize, saying 'Do you renounce?' or 'Do you believe?' The one who holds the child answers and says not 'He renounces' or 'He believes' like one speaking on behalf of another, but 'I renounce' or 'I believe'. This is the reason why little children can be called 'penitents' and 'believers'.

To certain who disapprove of this practice, the following reply is found from the Fathers. If children are not to be called 'penitents' because they have no awareness of repenting, nor should they be called believers because likewise they have no awareness of believing. But if they are rightly called believers because in a certain manner they profess faith through the words of those carrying them, why are they not previously held to be penitents when they are shown to renounce the devil and this world through the words of the same carriers? The whole of this is done in hope by the strength of the sacrament and divine grace which the Lord bestowed on the church. And when they are baptized by virtue of the power and celebration of so great a sacrament, although they do not do with their own heart and mouth what pertains to believing and confessing, nevertheless they are counted among the number of believers.

It has happened to many people when pressed by some extremity of death that, with a catholic mind and heart not alienated from the unity of peace, they rushed to some heretic and received Christ's baptism from him without receiving his aberration. Whether they died or recovered they never for a moment remained with those heretics to whom at heart they had never gone over. How can it happen that what one person confers to his ruin, another receives to his salvation, unless the sacrament received is judged according to the faith of the recipients and not according to the faith of the giver?

For this reason it comes about that those born deaf or mute are found in the ranks of catholics or heretics. So when the apostle says, 'How will they believe unless they hear?' (Romans 10:14) and 'Therefore faith comes from hearing' (Romans 10:17), nevertheless in a wonderful way, whether they are deaf or mute or infants, through the hearts and mouths of those who present and receive them they join the company of believers.[22]

This long exposition is truly a mixed bag, gathering together a handful of patristic testimonies of differing value. The first, however, is probably Leidrad's own contribution. It interestingly establishes that the child is addressed directly and answers directly through his carrier, but as an explanation why the child is called a believer it is merely formal. The second paragraph appeals generally to the power of the sacrament, but does not, for example, suggest this is a faith-imparting power. The third, from Augustine's anti-Donatist writings, is not only beside the point but even detrimental to it, with its useless punchline 'the sacrament received is judged according to the faith of the recipients'.[23] Finally, the analogy with the deaf and the mute runs up against obvious damaging objections.

Such a heterogeneous miscellany implies the difficulty, even the desperateness, of the position being justified. This lecture is more concerned to corroborate the facts of the situation than examine rationales for it. That so weak a mixture of reasons was resorted to by Leidrad for our purposes merely reinforces the deep-seated strength of the traditional and universal procedure.

---

[22] Keefe, *Water and the Word*, Vol. 2, 379–80. The analogy of the deaf and the mute was invoked by Isidore, *De ecclesiasticis officiis* 2:25:7, in *Corpus Christianorum* 113 (ed. C.M. Lawson; Turnhout: Brepols, 1989), 105.
[23] Cf. Augustine, *Baptism* 6:5:7, and for discussion, Wright, 'Donatist Theologoumena in Augustine?'.

We have seen how the English Reformers only marginally improved on late medieval practice. The Lutheran Reformation reveals a similar picture. Luther's first *Baptism Booklet* (*Taufbüchlein*) of 1523 has the blunt rubric '*Then the priest shall make the child through his godparents renounce the devil, saying*: N., dost thou renounce the devil?' This reproduces exactly what Luther found in his main source, the Magdeburg *Agenda* of 1497. Instead of 'I renounce', thrice, and 'I believe', thrice, in the Magdeburg book, Luther's text gives simply 'Yes' as the answer to all the questions. It was surely less demanding of the child.[24] Exactly the same, both rubric and answers, appeared in Luther's second *Baptism Booklet* of 1526, and also in the *Brandenburg-Nuremberg Church Order* of 1533, which had a wide-ranging influence on later German service books and even on the first English book of 1549.[25]

Within the Reformed variety of early Protestantism a happier situation developed. In general Reformed baptismal rites talked about the child and the faith of the church and then asked the parents(s) if they believed it, with the upbringing of the child in view. Strasbourg under Martin Bucer and his fellow Reformers was a creative nursery of liturgical reform. Until 1530 the only question, so to speak, asked during the baptism was this:

> You godparents and you brothers and sisters shall each of you teach this child Christian order, discipline and fear of God, each of you, as God gives him grace.
> *Answer*: We will.[26]

---

[24] J.D.C. Fisher, *Christian Initiation: The Reformation Period* (Alcuin Club Collections 51; London: SPCK, 1970), 15, 8.
[25] Ibid., 24, 29, 26.
[26] Ibid., 37.

Baptism and Profession of Faith

This is not carried forward into the Strasbourg orders from 1537 onwards, but there is a strengthened admonition to the godparents in the context of 'the whole community of the church', and before the Apostles' Creed is recited the ministers says:

> So now confess with me our holy Christian faith and thus arouse yourselves that you may grow valiant in the same and faithfully bring this infant (these children) up to share this faith.[27]

The Genevan order of baptism included in *La Forme des Prieres* of 1542 exemplifies the growing tendency of Reformed services, not solely of baptism, to major on exhortation and explanation. There are no questions of the traditional kind at all. After the Lord's Prayer the minister says:

> Since it is a matter of receiving this infant into the company of the Christian church, do you promise, when he comes to the age of discretion, to instruct him in the doctrine which is received among the people of God, as it is briefly summarized in the confession of faith which we all have.[28]

The declaration of the Creed which immediately follows apparently serves as the whole congregation's answering promise, with no role for godparents and no explicit part for the parents. Finally, in the first Scottish *Book of Common Order* of 1564, very closely based on the service used by John Knox in the English-speaking congregation in Geneva, the father and godfather present the child at the outset and are asked:

---

[27] Ibid., 41.
[28] Ibid., 116 (without a concluding question mark).

> Do you present this child to be baptized, earnestly desiring that he may be ingrafted in the mystical body of Jesus Christ?[29]

A routine question of this sort appears in all orders in every age. This one is notable for the strongly realist doctrine of baptism it conveys. This Knoxian service is heavily didactic and exhortatory, distinctive in requiring the father, or in his absence, the godfather, to 'rehearse the articles of his faith', that is, the Creed, after this instruction by the minister:

> [T]o the intent that we may be assured that you the father and the surety consent to the performance hereof, declare here before God and face of his congregation the sum of that faith, wherein you believe, and will instruct the child.[30]

The clean break with Catholic tradition which these Reformed rites represent illustrates the sharper radicalism of the Reformation in the broad Reformed stream, compared with Lutheran and Anglican patterns. The absence of the credal questions tends if anything to throw even greater weight on the Apostles' Creed as the church's faith, but we should remember that the traditional questions embodied that Creed in three parts, sometimes in shortened form. If the unreality of the child's responses is unambiguously abandoned, we should not miss the substantive doctrine of baptism the Reformed services inculcated. The exception to this was Zwingli in Zürich. After his earlier denial of infant baptism he acknowledged his error in mid-1525 and produced a drastically pared-down service with no Creed, no questions, no

---

[29] Ibid., 120 (modernized).
[30] Ibid., 122.

responsibility laid on parents and godparents and no doctrine of baptism recognizable in it at all.[31] Not a few modern Reformed churchmen and even theologians have leaned more towards Zwingli's baptismal minimalism than to the vigorous convictions of the Reformed mainstream, and sometimes without realizing it.

What of more recent practice? I will illustrate from the Church of England and the Church of Scotland, as representative of two quite different traditions, as we have seen, but tending in their published orders of service to display a genuine degree of convergence.

The Anglican *Alternative Service Book* of 1980 addressed the questions, in two groups of three, to the parents and godparents for them to answer 'for yourselves and for these children', but the answers are in the first person singular. The three questions about belief are credal in being Trinitarian, but not in content. Thus the second is, 'Do you believe and trust in his Son Jesus Christ, who redeemed mankind?', and the third, 'Do you believe and trust in the Holy Spirit, who gives life to the people of God?' The Apostles' Creed is not used in the service. It starts with the priest saying to parents and godparents:

> Christians who are too young to confess the Christian faith are baptized on the understanding that they are brought up as Christians within the family of the Church.

One attractive touch has the priest saying to a child 'old enough to understand':

> N, when you are baptized, you become a member of a new family. God takes you for his own child, and all Christian people will be your brothers and sisters.

---

[31] Ibid., 129–31.

58   *What has Infant Baptism done to Baptism?*

For the rest, such a child is treated throughout like other infants. When a family is baptized, 'children who are old enough to respond' may, at the discretion of the priest, answer the questions as well as the parents and godparents.[32]

Twenty years later in the Church of England's *Common Worship* (2000) the baptismal liturgy distinguishes prominently between those who are able to answer for themselves and those who are not. The questions, six of them, on renunciation and repentance and on turning and submitting to Christ, are addressed to 'the candidates directly, or through their parents, godparents and sponsors', and are answered by all of them in the first person singular, for example, 'I come to Christ'. The credal questions, on the other hand, are now directed to the whole congregation together with the candidates. The questions are one-liners: 'Do you believe and trust in God the Father? … in the Holy Spirit?' The answers in which all join contain the whole Apostles' Creed and are given in the first person singular. Only of a candidate able to answer for him/herself may the president then ask, by name, 'Is this your faith?', but this is awkward coming after the candidate has already joined in professing his/her faith in the Creed![33]

As the Church of England's long-considered new book of both traditional and contemporary services authorised to stand alongside the *Book of Common Prayer*, *Common Worship* enjoys lofty significance. That it should still be addressing questions to infants through adults strikes one as remarkable, not to say bizarre. It is also noteworthy that no special procedure at all for non-answering babies is

---

[32] *The Alternative Service Book 1980* (Oxford: Oxford University Press, 1984), 245–47, 243, 225.
[33] *Common Worship. Services and Prayers for the Church of England* (London: Church House Publishing, 2000), 353, 356, 357.

Baptism and Profession of Faith

provided for the credal profession of faith. The *Alternative Service Book* had retained an order specifically for 'The Baptism of Children', whereas *Common Worship* has a unitary baptismal service with internal alternatives. Both books place an order for thanksgiving for the gift of a child, in birth or adoption, before the baptism service. *Common Worship*'s treatment of infants is open to sharp criticism, perpetuating an element of vicarious unreality with questions directed to babies through adults. By contrast in the Catholic Church's infant baptism service approved in 1969 all of the ten questions are addressed to the parents and grandparents and answered by them in their own person.[34]

We look briefly at three versions of the Church of Scotland's *Book of Common Order*, 1928, 1940 and 1994. The brief service in 1928 addressed a single question to the parents:

> In presenting your child for baptism, do you anew profess your faith in Jesus Christ as your Lord and Saviour; and do you promise, in dependence on the grace of God, to bring up your child in the nurture and admonition of the Lord?[35]

By 1940 the service had expanded significantly, with now four questions to 'those who present the child', of which the first asks whether they 'receive the doctrine of the Christian Faith whereof we make confession, saying: I believe in God ...', but it is not clear if the presenters of babies join in declaring the Apostles' Creed, for they still have to answer 'I do'. The singular person doing the

---

[34] *The Rites of the Catholic Church*, Vol. 1 (Collegeville, MN: Liturgical Press, 1990), 401–402. This is a Study Edition of the Roman Ritual revised by the decree of the Second Vatican Council.
[35] *Book of Common Order 1928* (London: Oxford University Press, 1928), 40.

answering is each of the child's presenters speaking individually.[36]

The 1994 book is unusual for a service-book of this date in having separate baptismal services for children and for adults in that order. The one for children could be said to combine elements from 1928 and 1940. The minister asks the parents:

> In presenting your child for baptism, desiring that she may be grafted into Christ as a member of his body the Church, do you receive the teaching of the Christian faith which we confess in the Apostles' Creed?

Oddly enough, only after the parents' answer does the whole congregation declare the Apostles' Creed. After the baptism itself the parents are called, in question and answer, to promise to bring the child up in the Christian faith and church.[37]

This Church of Scotland 1994 *Book* betrays trends observable elsewhere in recent baptismal liturgies. First, a shift is discernible from requiring candidates or their sponsors actually to confess faith in God, Father, Son and Holy Spirit, to questioning them limply (parents in this case) whether they 'receive the teaching of the Christian faith'. The order for adult baptism is even less satisfactory, with this single question:

> In seeking baptism, do you reject sin, and confess your need of God's forgiving grace; and believing the Christian faith, do you pledge yourself to glorify God and to love your neighbour?[38]

---

[36] *Book of Common Order of the Church of Scotland* (London: Oxford University Press, 1940), 90–91.
[37] *Book of Common Order of the Church of Scotland* (Edinburgh: St Andrew Press, 1994), 87.
[38] Ibid., 99.

The declaration of the Creed which immediately follows is no longer tied to the candidate's vague 'believing the Christian faith' at all. From another perspective this is also a shift from the individual's personal confession to relying on the faith of the church.

The reasons behind these tendencies are not hard to seek. They reflect a desire to accommodate parents (the Church of Scotland makes no provision for godparents) who may not be comfortable confessing their own faith in Christ. 'Receiving the teaching of the Christian faith' is altogether less challenging. For adults 'believing the Christian faith' – at that point still unspecified – is a pale substitute for professing personal faith in Christ. These disappointing features in the 1994 *Book* may also be indicative of a growing emphasis on the way of the Christian as a pilgrimage with no firm starting point and in this life no attainable goal. So being a Christian has no decisive beginning, from non-faith in Christ to faith in Christ, but is a quest, a journey within faith, and also within non-faith and doubt.

Some writers, including a recent Faith and Order draft document, have taken to talking of baptism itself as lifelong, not merely with lifelong implications and outworkings, but itself in some sense a continuing unfinished experience.[39] This strange notion runs up against all kinds of objections, from Paul in Romans 6 to catholic order's interest in the validity of a baptism – and to plain common sense. One either has or has not been baptized at any one time.

It may seem surprising to some in this audience, and worse than surprising, that, of the recent English-language

---

[39] Cf. 'baptism is not a punctiliar event but a process of growth'; 'baptism as a life-long process of incorporation into Christ', *Becoming a Christian: The Ecumenical Implications of our Common Baptism* (report of a Faith and Order Consultation held at Faverges, France, 17–24 January 1997), paras. 36, 44.

service books surveyed here, by far the most satisfactory in its treatment of profession of faith in the case of infant baptism is the Roman Catholic rite. But as we shall see, this is not the only way in which that church is in the forefront of the renewal of baptismal belief and practice. Since it promises a further revision of its rite of infant baptism in the context of the recovery of the catechumenate, more good news may be expected.

This lecture belongs to a series enquiring into the damage infant baptism has done to baptism. In respect of profession of faith infant-baptism services at the present day disclose perhaps greater variety than at any time in church history. The Anglican *Common Worship* (2000) perpetuates the incongruity of questioning babies and extracting answers from them through their sponsors. The Roman Catholic Church has at last decisively broken with this ventriloquist charade, while the Church of Scotland has virtually abandoned the questions of hallowed baptismal tradition, despite its continuing if awkward use of the Apostles' Creed, and seems still to have allowed the form for baptizing babies to influence the one for adults. Purging the body ecclesiastical of the detrimental effects of infant baptism's long reign has still some distance to go.

3

Baptism in Mission

Catechumenate and Discipleship

A major difference between narratives of baptism in the New Testament, chiefly the Acts of the Apostles, and the developing picture from the second and later centuries is the period of catechumenate before baptism. The Greek verb κατηχέω means 'instruct' (it is a compound of which the second part gives us the word 'echo'), and so the catechumen is a person under instruction. 'Catechesis' is used, like 'catechumenate', of the programme and also of the teaching content, and the catechist is a teacher of catechumens, whom he catechizes.

The church of the Fathers took preparation for baptism seriously – extraordinarily seriously, we might think. According to the *Apostolic Tradition* attached to the name of Hippolytus, the catechumenate normally lasted three years, and another source hints that it may in some case have extended to five years.[1] The contrast with the more or less immediate baptisms in Acts, in Jerusalem, Philippi and elsewhere, is inescapable. Of course we have no statistics attesting how many catechumens waited three years, but we can cite three factors that could shorten the time. First, during the period before Constantine, when a

---

[1] Hippolytus, *Apostolic Tradition* 17:1, Bradshaw et al., *Apostolic Tradition*, 96–98, for other evidence and discussion.

serious prospect of persecution loomed the catechumens were baptized promptly, in order that the gift of the Holy Spirit received through baptism might stiffen them to endure the pains of persecution without surrendering. (If catechumens were martyred, their 'blood-baptism' covered their lack of water-baptism. The phrase was widely used of martyrdom.) Secondly, the Hippolytan work itself tells us, immediately after stipulating that the catechumens 'hear the Word for three years', that

> [I[f one is earnest and perseveres well in the work, the time is never judged, but the character only is that which shall be judged.[2]

Thirdly, the growing tendency for baptisms to take place at Easter, or within the Easter season up to Pentecost, would itself have encouraged an overall one-year rather than three-year norm, such as we observe in the case of Augustine in the *Confessions*.

Nevertheless, speedy baptism was a thing of the apostolic past, being attested in the patristic era only in an emergency of some kind, such as the threat of persecution, grave illness or natural or military disaster. The abandonment of such rapid baptism probably had something to do with the shift in recruitment from Jews to Gentiles, who not only needed basic theistic and ethical instruction which Jewish converts should not have needed but also required purification and release from the defilements of pagan idolatry.[3]

---

[2] Hippolytus, *Apostolic Tradition* 17:2, Bradshaw et al., *Apostolic Tradition*, 96.

[3] Bradshaw et al., *Apostolic Tradition*, 98, point out that the Council of Nicaea in 325 AD still 'sought to ensure that a period of adequate preparation for baptism be provided in order to guarantee that the transition from pagan to Christian life not be as abrupt as apparently it had been previously'. The reference is to canon 2.

The feature of the baptismal and pre-baptismal rites in the *Apostolic Tradition* which appears most astonishing to modern readers is the frequency of exorcisms. It encouraged William Willimon to call this a 'detoxification' exercise.[4] That is to say, exorcisms were part of a lengthy procedure which deconstructed pagans and reconstructed them as Christians. It was a deliberate endeavour to ensure the re-formation of pagans as Christians, 'to resocialize them … so that they would emerge as Christian people who would be at home in communities of freedom'.[5]

The process, or the programme as it might with a deliberate Tendenz be called, had built into it a series of check-ups at which candidates' advancement could be halted if progress had been insufficient. To cite an analogy in the *Spiritual Exercises* of Ignatius Loyola would be an exaggeration, but it bespeaks a purposeful concern for a disciplined re-making of a person which calls to mind the more self-consciously formulated schemes for discipling new converts which are a feature of some areas of modern evangelicalism. This similarity may not be accidental if the missionary task of the churches in Britain today demands a more sharply focussed attention on stripping out the grip of a deeply de-Christianized, if not truly pagan, culture on those making their way into the Christian community.

It is not difficult to cite contemporary case studies which illustrate the timeliness of revisiting early Christian practice. A couple were converted through an Alpha course and seemed to be settling well into the church. In due course they requested baptism – and were deeply upset to discover that the church would not baptize them

---

[4] Quoted by Alan Kreider, *Worship and Evangelism in Pre-Christendom* (Alcuin/GROW Joint Liturgical Studies 32; Cambridge: Grove Books, 1995), 26, citing William H. Willimon, *Peculiar Speech: Preaching to the Baptized* (Grand Rapids, MI: Eerdmans, 1992), 59.

[5] Kreider, *Worship and Evangelism*, 23.

unless they first got married. They had hitherto picked up no suggestion that living together unmarried was at all problematic for their Christian discipleship. In the early church this was exactly the kind of disqualification that would have been identified in the initial scrutiny of occupations and relationships when someone first sought admission to the catechumenate.[6] It was recently a matter of internal debate whether, if an applicant for the ordained ministry in a particular mainline denomination in Britain disclosed during the selection process that he or she was living together with a member of the opposite sex unmarried or with a member of the same sex, this would be sufficient of itself to debar progress. My immediate reflection recalled that, in a church ordered according to the *Apostolic Tradition*, such a person would not be accepted as a catechumen for training for baptism, let alone ordination.

One thing is plain from the *Apostolic Tradition*, backed up by the contemporary North African writer Tertullian and the later Origen, that the gate of baptism was strictly guarded in those early centuries. The clear impression is given that passage was not secured without stringent enquiry and examination. It is almost as if getting into the church was of set purpose made a demanding exercise. The periodically hostile environment partly explains this fencing of the baptismal waters, but despite the almost deterrent force of the regulations for the catechumenate, it belonged to a church which grew year on year at a highly commendable rate. Statistically, the church of the Fathers was an undoubted success story, but it succeeded without opening the doors wide and welcoming allcomers with a warm embrace and no questions asked. On the growth of

---

[6] See Hippolytus, *Apostolic Tradition* 16, Bradshaw et al., *Apostolic Tradition*, 88–95.

the early church a revealing and generally reliable analysis is to be found in *The Rise of Christianity* by the eminent American sociologist Rodney Stark.[7]

If, then, entry to the Christian community was rigorously monitored with baptism in view, what happened when infants were baptized? Apart from the obvious answer that they were not taken through three years, or even one year, of 'hearing the Word', as the *Apostolic Tradition* summarizes the catechumenate, we know very little. One thing which seems not to have existed in this numerically fast-expanding early church was what today would be subsumed under 'children's ministries'. We have hints and glimpses sufficient to justify the assumption that youngsters were taught and trained in the Christian faith, but mostly in the context of the family, it seems.[8]

The invisibility of church youth and children's work cannot have had anything to do with paucity of offspring among Christians. One of the most original sections in Rodney Stark's book is entitled 'The Fertility Factor', which he found hardly ever discussed in investigations of the expansion of early Christianity. The conclusion Stark reaches is that Christians bred more prolifically than pagans:

> On the one hand Christians did not resort to practices that contributed to demographic decline in the Greco-Roman world, such as abortion, infanticide, exposure of unwanted children, especially baby girls, birth control, including contraceptive devices and nonreproductive forms of sexual

---

[7] Rodney Stark, *The Rise of Christianity* (Princeton, NJ: Princeton University Press, 1996). For scholarly evaluation see the articles in the *Journal of Early Christian Studies* 6:2 (1998).

[8] For an introduction see David F. Wright, 'A Family Faith: Domestic Discipling', in *Bibliotheca Sacra* 160 (2003), 259–68.

congress. On the other hand the ranks of Christianity contained 'an abundance of fertile women,' perhaps 60 percent or more of its membership.[9]

The oversupply of Christian women, especially at the upper social level, led to more mixed marriages than Christian writers like Tertullian could tolerate, but the general verdict is that most of the products of these Christian-pagan unions were brought up as Christians. Augustine is a notable example.

In the long term, the universality of baby baptism resulted in the transposition of the catechumenate after baptism, which was the Sitz im Leben for the numerous catechisms compiled in the Protestant Reformations of the sixteenth century. The standard structural framework of these catechisms was provided by the Apostles' Creed, the Lord's Prayer, the Ten Commandments and often the sacraments of the gospel. Catechizing typically issued in the young person's profession of faith prior to admission to the Lord's Table through a ceremony like modern confirmation.

But although the noun 'catechism' seems to have been first used of such handbooks of basic Christian teaching in the early sixteenth century, the custom of instructing the young in the faith was well established in the later medieval centuries. Thus the *Sarum Manual*, the Salisbury service book widely used in England before the Reformation, ordered at the end of its form for baptism that

> the godmothers should be enjoined to teach the infant the Our Father, and Hail Mary, and I believe in God, or cause them to be taught them.[10]

---

[9] Ibid., 262–63, citing Stark, *Rise of Christianity*, 126.
[10] Fisher, *Christian Initiation: Baptism in the Medieval West*, 175.

A variety of short texts or summaries could be enlisted to give a framework for such catechizing, including the seven Beatitudes, the seven gifts of the Holy Spirit, the seven deadly sins, the seven chief virtues and the seven works of mercy, along with the Decalogue. So the Reformers' catechisms built on Catholic antecedents, and hundreds of pastors in the reformed churches compiled catechisms for their own use which never attained the prominence of Luther's small *Catechism* and never made it into print.[11]

Yet the *Sarum Manual*'s post-baptismal rubrics, in laying down guidance for baptisms at Easter and Pentecost, require that 'during the interval between the birth of the children and their baptism they receive the complete catechism'.[12] On turning back to the baptism service itself, one finds that the first main part, occupying over seven pages in Fisher's translation, is entitled 'The Order for the Making of a Catechumen'.[13] It comprises a range of prayers, ritual actions, adjurations and instructions which together provide a concentrated catechumenate – all transacted over the baby in rapid succession at the church door. At the end of this preliminary section, the priest is directed to

> introduce the catechumen by the right hand into the church, having asked his (or her) name, saying:
> N. enter into the temple of God, that thou mayest have eternal life, and live for ever and ever. Amen.[14]

---

[11] For such catechisms see Gerald Strauss, *Luther's House of Learning. Indoctrination of the Young in the German Reformation* (Baltimore: Johns Hopkins University Press, 1978).
[12] Fisher, *Christian Initiation: Baptism in the Medieval West*, 177.
[13] Ibid., 158–65.
[14] Ibid., 165.

This 'Order for the Making of a Catechumen' includes five separate signings of the cross on the child, four on the forehead and one on the hand, an exorcism, the placing of a pinch of salt in the child's mouth after the salt has itself been exorcized, and the reciting by the godparents and others present of the Lord's Prayer, Hail Mary and Apostles' Creed, after the infant has received the Ephphatha, or Effeta. This last ritual is based on Jesus' actions and word in healing the deaf and mute man in Mark 7:31–35. The priest spits in his left hand and touches the ears and nose of the child with words suggesting their being opened to the teaching of the faith. This ritual comes after the only passage of Scripture to be read in this church-door procedure, the Matthaean version of Jesus' Blessing of the Children.[15]

What we observe here is the extraordinary persistence of the principle that accommodated the youngest of children within arrangements made for responsible participants, in this case not in baptism itself but in the pre-baptismal catechumenate. Babies who could, simply in physical terms, be baptized, i.e. passively dipped in or doused with water, but who could not answer the questions themselves, were put through the catechumenate, originally in the weeks of Lent prior to Easter. Reserving baptisms for Easter or Pentecost was easily feasible with older candidates, but with baby recipients it could just as easily become the exception. The rubric in the *Sarum Manual* noted above, requiring that between birth and baptism children 'receive the complete catechism', in fact refers to those born within eight days of Easter or of Pentecost, who 'must be reserved for baptism on Easter Eve or on the vigil of Pentecost'.[16] So a token attempt was made to preserve the special baptismal season. But the concentration of

---

[15] Ibid., 164.
[16] Ibid., 177.

elements from the catechumenate into the church-door 'Making of a Catechumen' reveals yet another absurdity resulting from the half-baked takeover of the baptismal function of the church's life by the newborn.

The key transitional phases of this takeover can be discerned in or deduced from two documents which 'witness to the ritual structure of Roman initiatory practice in the seventh and eighth centuries',[17] known as the *Gelasian Sacramentary* and *Ordo Romanus XI*. In both of these infants are envisaged as the normal recipients of baptism, and yet the ingredients of the pre-baptismal catechumenate developed for responsible participants are pressed into service with as little disruption as possible. Just one example must suffice. Candidates for baptism were subjected during their catechumenal preparation to what became known as 'scrutinies' (Latin, *scrutinium*). These were assessments to determine 'whether any aspects of their lives still needed to be set free from the influence of sin and evil'.[18] Here is the *Apostolic Tradition*'s primitive description of such testings:

> And from the time that they will be separated, let hand be laid on them daily, exorcising them. And when the day draws near when they will be baptized, let the bishop exorcise each one of them so that he may know that they are holy.
>
> But if there is one who is not good or undefiled, let him be put aside because he did not hear the Word faithfully, since it is never possible to hide the stranger.[19]

---

[17] Johnson, *Rites of Christian Initiation*, 180.

[18] Maxwell E. Johnson, 'Scrutinies, Baptismal', in Paul Bradshaw (ed.), *The New SCM Dictionary of Liturgy and Worship* (London: SCM Press, 2002), 427.

[19] Hippolytus, *Apostolic Tradition* 20:3–4, Bradshaw et al., *Apostolic Tradition*, 104, 108, with the editors' comment that 'stranger' here probably betrays an original reference to the devil.

This passage comes from the version in the Sahidic language, one of the forms of Egyptian Coptic. The Ethiopic text makes no mention of exorcism at all.[20] By the time of the Gelasian and Roman orders, the scrutinies have become highly formalized and, with infants as their subjects, have lost touch with the original sense of 'scrutiny' and been reduced to 'little more than solemn exorcisms of infant "catechumens"'.[21] When the weeks of Lent were further compressed into the church-door ceremony, the scrutinies were even more remote from their original investigative role.

One feature of this infant-dominated descent into unreality deserves special mention. It seems that it was in the course of this regressive development, during the seventh and eighth centuries more precisely, that the Gospel incident of Jesus' blessing of little children was recruited to justify the laying of hands on infant heads in the remnants of the catechumenate now conscripted to process infants.[22] At the time when, as witnessed in the *Gelasian Sacramentary*, the scrutinies took place on the third, fourth and fifth Sundays in Lent, there is evidence that all three Synoptic versions of the Gospel pericope were used for these occasions. In *Sarum*'s church-door ceremony, Matthew was the preferred version. It is important to stress that there is hardly any trace of this passage being used or interpreted in connexion with infant baptism in the patristic period. This should not surprise us, since we have seen that early Christian baptism as a liturgical order was

---

[20] Bradshaw et al., *Apostolic Tradition*, 109.
[21] Johnson, 'Scrutinies, Baptismal', 427.
[22] For what follows see David F. Wright, 'Out, In, Out: Jesus' Blessing of the Children and Infant Baptism', in Stanley E. Porter and Anthony R. Cross (eds.), *Dimensions of Baptism. Biblical and Theological Studies* (Journal for the Study of the New Testament Suppl. Ser. 234; London, New York: Sheffield Academic Press, 2002), 188–206.

focussed on candidates able to answer for themselves, and that the incorporation of candidates carried in parental arms occasioned minimal adjustment of the rite.

The sixteenth-century Reformers did away with the church-door preliminaries, partly by abandoning unworthy, that is, unbiblical elements, and partly by bringing acceptable ones in out of the cold, into the service of baptism itself which ideally should take place, so most of them insisted, in the face of the congregation. (Hence the symbolic significance of having the font at the back of the church just inside the door yielded to the didactic value of placing it in full view of all at the front.) And so Reformation baptism texts generally include Jesus' Blessing of the Children as scriptural reading and helpful justification.

The process of transition is visible in the successive editions of the *Book of Common Prayer*. The first, in 1549, retained, but now in English, much of *Sarum*'s church-door procedures, including the Gospel pericope but in the Markan version, in this detail reflecting Lutheran influence.[23] The retention of the artificial church-door preliminary, now by Cranmer unhooked from any explicit link with the catechumenate, was heavily criticized by Martin Bucer in his *Censura* of the 1549 book.[24] So the 1552 revision located the whole service at the font, but kept the Markan passage early on, together also with the following exhortation based on it, also from the 1549 book, which served as an apologia for the baptizing of infants.[25] Thus this Gospel episode was launched on a new career as a key scriptural and indeed dominical support for the practice of

---

[23] *First and Second Prayer-Books*, 236–39.
[24] See the extract in Fisher, *Christian Initiation: The Reformation Period*, 98.
[25] *First and Second Prayer-Books*, 394–96.

baptizing babies, a career which would last until the later years of the twentieth century.

We have tracked, largely in this lecture by attending to the texts of Western baptismal development, a truly massive change in the history of Christ's church. From being a company recruited by intentional response to the gospel imperative to discipleship and baptism, it became a body enrolled from birth. It was arguably one of the greatest sea changes in the story of Christianity. It led, as we have seen, to the formation of Christendom, comprising a Christian empire, Christian nations or peoples. Christianity became a matter of heredity, not decision.[26] The famous and telling words of Tertullian, *fiunt, non nascuntur, Christiani*, 'people are made, not born, Christians', were turned upside down. 'People become Christians, they are not born already Christians.' Tertullian was, of course, the earliest known opponent of baby baptism, but it was not in this context that he penned this powerful dictum. Rather it occurs in one of his greatest works, the *Apology*. Addressing pagan readers, he had been talking about the messengers God sent into the world to proclaim that there was only one true God, creator, providential ruler of the earth, judge of all at the consummation:

> Once these things were with us, too, the theme of ridicule. We are of your stock and nature; people are made, not born, Christians.[27]

It was pagans who were made into Christians. This making of Christians out of pagans had a powerful centre in baptism in the time of Tertullian. The administration of

---

[26] Cf. Walter Hobhouse, *The Church and the World in Idea and History* (Bampton Lectures 1909; London: MacMillan and Co., 1911²), 66–67.
[27] Tertullian, *Apology* 18.

baptism, with its careful programme of preparatory formation, was an important instrument of mission. In his treatise on *Baptism*, where he takes his stand against the baptism of infants, Tertullian writes, with contextual reference to Jesus' words, 'Forbid them not to come to me' (Mt. 19:14):

> So let them come, when they are growing up (*adolescunt*), when they are learning, when they are being taught what they are coming to: let them be made (*fiant*) Christians when they have become competent (*potuerint*, 'able') to know Christ. Why should innocent infancy come with haste to the remission of sins? Shall we take less cautious action in this than we take in worldly matters? Shall one who is not entrusted with earthly property be entrusted with heavenly? Let them first learn how to ask for salvation, so that you may be seen to have given to one who asks (cf. Mt 5:42).[28]

This oft-quoted but still in some respects puzzling text puts baptism in the setting of making disciples, but with a distinctive twist as far as most modern evangelicals are concerned. 'Let them be made Christians when they have become able to know Christ'. For Tertullian being 'made Christians' means being baptized. Earlier in this book he states in so many words, 'Now there is a standing rule that without baptism no one can obtain salvation. This derives in particular from that pronouncement of the Lord, who says, "Except a person be born of water, he cannot have life".'[29]

According to the imagery of the New Testament writings, which was further enriched among the Fathers,

---

[28] Tertullian, *Baptism* 18:5, in *Tertullian's Homily on Baptism* (trans. Ernest Evans; London: SPCK, 1964), 39.
[29] Tertullian, *Baptism*, 12:1, in *Tertullian's Homily on Baptism*, 27, adapted.

baptism itself was the occasion, the experience of transition. This illustrates the productive fertility of baptism in early Christianity. It marked the passage through burial in death to risen life in Christ (Rom. 6:3–14), dramatically symbolized by being plunged beneath the water and emerging out of it again. Linked with this dimension of immersion is the baptismal experience of stripping off the old identity and being reclothed with the new, even with Christ himself (Gal. 3:27; Col. 3:9, 12). The white garments of the newly baptized spoke of their cleansing from sin through baptism. Consonant with this divesting oneself of the old nature, the old person, is the image of baptism as rebirth: 'He saved us through the washing of rebirth and renewal by the Holy Spirit' (Tit. 3:5). There is also the transition from one human solidarity – 'in Adam' – to another: 'We were all baptized by one Spirit into one body – whether Jews or Greeks, slave or free – and we were all given the one Spirit to drink' (1 Cor. 12:13).

Perhaps building on Paul's cue in 1 Corinthians 10:1–2, the Fathers developed a paschal interpretation of baptism which again embodied transition. 'Our forefathers were all under the cloud and … all passed through the sea. They were all baptized into Moses in the cloud and the sea.' The Hebrew (and Aramaic) word for 'passover', *pesah*, was transliterated in Greek as πάσχα, which furnished the standard Greek and Latin word for Easter, a festival celebrating not merely the resurrection of Christ but his crucifixion and burial also. The Pascha was the first great festival of the emerging Christian calendar. Sorting out the sequence of influence and dependence is not a simple matter, but, as noted already, the Christian Pascha became the proper season for baptism, which in itself, quite apart from the imagery this fostered, spoke eloquently of the significance of baptism. In baptism men and women 'passed over' from death to life through water, from the old order of Egypt to the new of the Promised Land, from the seventh day (the sabbath) to the eighth day, which is also the first day, the Lord's day, the day of resurrection and baptismal renewal. As baptisms took place early on Easter morning, so they also symbolized the transition from darkness to light.

Much of what we have been discussing meant that baptism was a drama, a dramatic enactment of both the gift of God's grace in Christ and human response to it in faith. It is one of the sad legacies of the long reign of infant baptism that it has shrunk baptism even as an action or drama. Karl Barth's critique of infant baptism in the 1940s spoke of 'the innocuous form of present-day baptism':

> One can hardly deny that baptism carried out as immersion ... showed what was represented in far more expressive fashion than did the affusion which later became customary, especially when this affusion was reduced from a real wetting to a sprinkling and eventually in practice to a mere moistening with as little water as possible.[30]

And that concerns only the quantity of the water!

If we follow the direction of theological and practical movement which is indicated by taking faith baptism as the norm, then we should fasten our attention first on the rite for believers and only then consider how appropriately to handle infants. The burden of my argument at this point rests on the present-day potential in the catechumenate leading up to baptism, yes, even on Easter Sunday, for the ongoing Christian mission of making disciples.

One of the most interesting texts in the area of Christian initiation produced in recent years is the Roman Catholic

---

[30] Barth, *The Teaching of the Church Regarding Baptism*, 9–10.

Church's *Rite of Christian Initiation of Adults*, often referred to as *RCIA*. The Latin text was first published in 1972, and in an emended version in 1974, from which the final English translation of 1985 was made. This was authorized for use in the United States in the edition of 1988.[31] The Second Vatican Council decreed the revision of the rite of baptism of adults and the restoration of the catechumenate for adults.[32] The result is *RCIA*, a weighty volume of over 350 pages. Here you will find many of the elements we have taken note of in this lecture: exorcisms, the three scrutinies, the Ephphatha rite, provision for a variable duration of the catechumenate ('long enough – several years if necessary – for the conversion and faith of the catechumens to become strong'),[33] baptism by immersion (of the whole body or of the head alone) or by 'pouring' water three times on the candidate's bowed head, credal questions close to the pattern and wording in the *Apostolic Tradition*, clothing with a baptismal garment, and presentation to the candidate of a lighted candle. Also included here is a whole parallel schema for unbaptized children who have reached catechetical age. And there is much else besides.

The *RCIA* and more broadly 'the Copernican revolution in sacramental theology today'[34] in Roman Catholicism, which *RCIA* both expressed and promoted, have been of enormous influence far beyond the Catholic Church. This is the judgement of Maxwell Johnson:

---

[31] *Rite of Christian Initiation of Adults* (study edn; Chicago: Liturgy Training Publications, 1988). The *Rite* itself is contained also in *The Rites of the Catholic Church*, Vol. 1 (Collegeville, MN: Liturgical Press, 1990), 13–356.

[32] Vatican Council II, 'Constitution on the Sacred Liturgy (*Sacrosanctum concilium*)', 64, 66, in *Vatican Council II: The Conciliar and Post Conciliar Documents* (trans Austin Flannery; Collegeville, MN: Liturgical Press, 1980²), 21.

[33] *Rite of Christian Initiation of Adults*, 38.

[34] Johnson, *Rites of Christian Initiation*, 306.

There is no question but that the dominant and most ecumenically influential of the modern reforms of the rites of Christian initiation have been those of the Roman Catholic Church, especially the RCIA. Understood by many as the most mature fruit of all the liturgical reforms mandated by the Second Vatican Council, it is this Roman Catholic restoration of the adult catechumenate and especially the recovery of the integral and unitive sequence of baptism, confirmation and first communion in the RCIA which clearly underlie all of the modern liturgical revisions of Christian initiation in other churches.[35]

That unitive sequence has not been part of my concern in these lectures, but I would like to commend the restored catechumenate in *RCIA* as worthy of careful study by all who are concerned with making Christian disciples in the contemporary world. It is, of course, of an entirely different order of activity from Alpha or similar courses. (I wonder what might emerge from some cross-fertilisation.) The doctrine it presupposes in *RCIA* is that of the Catholic faith, yet its Christ-centredness is inescapable. Here are a couple of quotations from the introduction to the catechumenate in *RCIA*:

> [T]he catechumens learn to turn more readily to God in prayer, to bear witness to the faith, in all things to keep their hopes set on Christ, to follow supernatural inspiration in their deeds, and to practice love of neighbor, even at the cost of self-renunciation.[36]

> The instruction that the catechumens receive during this period should be of a kind that while presenting Catholic teaching in its entirety also enlightens faith, directs the heart

---

[35] Ibid., 296.
[36] *Rite of Christian Initiation of Adults*, 37.

towards God, fosters participation in the liturgy, inspires apostolic activity, and nurtures a life completely in accord with the spirit of Christ.[37]

But if so much store is set on the restored catechumenate, what about infant baptism after its release from the domination of Christendom? Several things may be said. First, infants are to be treated as infants, and not 'as mute adults'.[38] If that should seem self-evidently right to most of us, we should remember that the Second Vatican Council found it necessary to rule that:

> The rite for the baptism of infants is to be revised, its revision taking into account that those to be baptized are infants.[39]

All trace of vicarious renunciation and profession of faith by sponsors, as though by some form of ventriloquism, must be abandoned. This means, secondly, that the faith that is called for is that of parents, godparents or other sponsors and of the church community as a whole. As we saw in the second lecture, no recent rite exemplifies this so clearly as the Roman Catholic rite. Thirdly, indiscriminate administration and all unnecessary haste must be avoided. The introduction to the Catholic service states that:

> In the complete absence of any well-founded hope that the infant will be brought up in the Catholic religion, the baptism is to be delayed … and the parents are to be informed of the reasons.[40]

---

[37] Ibid., 38.
[38] Johnson, *Rites of Christian Initiation*, 319.
[39] *Constitution on the Sacred Liturgy*, 67, in *Vatican Council II*, 21.
[40] *The Rites of the Catholic Church*, Vol. 1, 369.

Infant baptism is prospective in a manner additional to what is true also of believers' baptism, and a great deal must hinge on the Christian commitment of parents and perhaps others, such as godparents or other close relatives. It is also with the post-Vatican II rites of baptism that the Catholic tradition has at last virtually abandoned the insistence on newborn babies being baptized *quam primum*, 'as soon as possible'. Now it is the duty of parents to consult with the priest as soon as possible after the child's birth about baptism.[41]

In the fourth place, if infant baptism is to be given in the conviction that it is indeed baptism in the New Testament sense, it is essentially a reality which infants must grow into and which they must be brought up continually aware of. Thus baptism should be an important reference point of familial and Sunday school instruction. The Church of Scotland's *Book of Common Order* (1994) has a rather fine address to the parents after a child has been baptized:

> Your child belongs to God in Christ. From this day she will be at home in the Christian community, and there will always be a place for her. Tell her of her baptism, and unfold to her the treasure she has been given today, so that she may know she is baptized, and, as she grows, make her own response in faith and love, and come in due time to share in the communion of the body and blood of Christ.[42]

The Puritans used to speak about 'improving' one's baptism, and each baptism is very widely seen among the churches today as an occasion for the renewal of the baptismal experience and commitment of the baptized.[43]

---

[41] Johnson, *Rites of Christian Initiation*, 320–21.
[42] *Book of Common Order of the Church of Scotland* (1994), 90.
[43] This note is sounded from the earliest Scottish *Book of Common Order* (1564; cf. *The Liturgy of John Knox*, 156: 'it is not only of necessitie that we

Infant baptism in many churches has to be rescued from being more a family occasion than a church event, and so has to be saved from sentimentality and baby worship.[44] Maxwell Johnson notes that while explicit language about 'original sin' is nowhere evident in the *Rite of Christian Initiation of Adults*, it appears clearly in the Catholic rite of infant baptism. He comments:

> While such a theology is not dominant throughout the rite, its presence here certainly underscores the traditional inheritance of the Augustinian rationale *for* infant baptism itself.[45]

You may be asking, however, whether baptism merits the weight that I have been placing on it. That the church's practice of baptism was mandated by Christ himself with a clarity shared by very few other things we do in church is a good starting point in answering such a question. It is not at all obvious to me that Christ's authority lies behind the sermon, for example. But the question remains not only a serious one but even fundamental to these lectures, and the last lecture will be devoted to my response.

---

[43] (*continued*) be once baptised, but also it moch profiteth oft to be present at the ministration thereof') to the most recent, 1994: 'Gracious God, touch us all again this day with the grace of our baptism' (*Book of Common Order*, 107).

[44] Cf. my reflections on 'Habitats of Infant Baptism', in Wallace M. Alston, Jr. (ed.), *Theology in the Service of the Church. Essays in Honor of Thomas W. Gillespie* (Grand Rapids, MI: Eerdmans, 2000), 254–65.

[45] Johnson, *The Rites*, 320 (his italics).

4

Baptism

Effective Sign, or Merely Symbolic?

One of the aspects of baptism which makes it a congenial topic for an historian is that the claims made for it, even the actual doctrine of baptism, are to some degree empirically or historically verifiable. This is not true of, for example, the eucharist or Lord's supper. Indeed, the Catholic dogma of transubstantiation, which must be the most exalted of sacramental claims, by the very definition itself is totally unverifiable; the substance of the bread and wine is changed into the body and blood of Christ but their accidents – sight, colour, texture, touch, taste, weight – remain unchanged. The dogmatic truth claim of transubstantiation is by its very nature accessible only to faith. But on a more general level of eucharistic belief, if I were to test the doctrine that believers feed on Christ spiritually in the supper it would be extremely tricky verifying the claim. More straightforward would be a claim that marriage creates in some sense an indissoluble bond between husband and wife, although again the Roman Catholic Church excludes the possibility of divorce in a correctly contracted and consummated marriage, so that what might seem a dissolution of the bond to most observers is by such dogma declared to be truly impossible.

Of baptism it is commonly claimed that its recipients are incorporated into the body of Christ, become members of the church. In the Scottish *Book of Common Order* (1994) the minister says after the actual baptism that 'We receive and welcome her/him as a member of the one, holy, catholic and apostolic Church'.[1] (Oddly enough, the service is not so explicit about the child's becoming a member of the Church of Scotland! The lesser does not seem to follow from the greater – or is it encompassed within the greater? Perhaps membership of a church has sufficient administrative aspects to it not to be appropriately dealt with in a baptism service.) Now unless this assertion about being received as a member of the one church is given such a spiritual or metaphysical meaning that its truthfulness is wholly inaccessible to the social scientist or historian, it must surely entail membership of the visible church on earth. It would be strange, would it not, if, of hundreds of baptized persons of whom this was predicated over a period of time, none was subsequently found 'in church', at worship or engaged in some essential church activity. I am not forgetting that evangelical Christians have traditionally made much of the doctrine of the invisible church, but we should be cautious to summon this into play at this juncture. What this unfortunately named doctrine really stands for is the important biblical teaching that only God knows those who are his and that not all in the visible company of the church thereby truly belong to God. The doctrine of the invisible church is not about a totally different entity from the visible church – except insofar as it embraces those who have died and joined the heavenly host of God. It is at base a statement, paradoxically enough, about the visible church, affirming its mixed, imperfect character. I reject its being invoked to accommodate the embarrassing verifiable results of hundreds, thousands, even millions of infant baptisms which have

---

[1] *Book of Common Order of the Church of Scotland* (1994), 90.

not led to their recipients being verifiably members of the church of Jesus Christ.

Let us not beat about the bush. I am not aware of figures about believers' baptisms (but shall be very glad to be put out of my ignorance), but I know that they too are quite capable of leading nowhere in terms of active church membership. My subject is infant baptism, and any statistics can be only approximate. (I wonder if any paedobaptizing church or denomination has traced infant by infant the future spiritual fortunes of the infant-baptized over an appropriate time span. Again, I am eager to learn.) The necessary statistical exercise, in a church like the Church of Scotland which has for long had a fairly clear measure of membership by admission to communion on profession of faith is not difficult, in principle at any rate. It is in fact complicated for the Church of Scotland by two major church unions, in 1900 and 1929, and by the effects of two world wars in the twentieth century. A professional statistician would build in other variables, such as the impact of emigration and changes in the average age at which people become communicant members. Yet when all the caveats and qualifications have been factored in, there are undoubtedly hordes more people who were baptized as infants in the Church of Scotland and are today to all intents and purposes wholly unchurched than there are members of the same church – and here I use 'members' in an official sense, of all those who have once become communicant members and remain so. This paper membership itself has only a partial purchase on reality; the rule of thumb in the Kirk is that, of the formal membership in any one congregation, a third are active, another third come to special services like communion and Easter, and a third are never seen.

I doubt if the picture in the Church of England would be better – in fact, I am sure that it would be decidedly worse, both because paedobaptism has been legally more indiscriminate than in Scotland and because decline has affected the national church more severely in England than north of the border. Since the Church of England lacks a formal membership parallel to that in the Scottish Kirk, calculations would be more hazardous, although confirmations might be taken as a substitute measure. I wonder how different the picture would be in the Methodist Church, or for that matter in any other mainstream mixed denomination which baptizes babies. In my first lecture I touched on the Swedish Lutheran Church which baptizes still an astonishingly high percentage of the newborn yet assembles for worship a percentage of the population far smaller even than in England. The picture, we may be sure, is broadly the same in many countries, but especially where there is or has been a national or established church, that is, where Christendom has been the order of the day.

The state of affairs thus exposed confronts infant baptism with some hard questions. Some of its champions take exception to talk of the infant baptized now being in any realistic reckoning unchurched, and they may resort to inclusive ecclesiologies of one kind or another to encompass them, or indeed to inclusive theologies for which the church has no boundaries and infant baptism embodies the universal love of God that knows no limits and is never thwarted. These are escape routes which biblical Christians can scarcely take seriously. For them the outcome of considering this legacy of Christendom is more likely to be a dismal estimate of the effectiveness of infant baptism.

If for so many infants baptism which is initiation – the word derives from the Latin *initium*, meaning 'beginning'

– into the church, even into Christ, turns out to be a dead-end leading nowhere, what can we credibly affirm about its efficacy? We might conclude that for some who minister in one of these mixed churches the price of continuing to dispense baptism to babies is not believing too much about it. This is hardly a satisfactory position to find oneself in, but then the administration of infant baptism has been for some time one of the most conscience-taxing aspects of the work of the ministry for many evangelicals.

So again we come back to this massive baptismal reductionism which the long reign of infant baptism has inflicted on baptism. A vicious circle is at work. A low view of infant baptism condones or even plays along with a no-questions-asked policy of generous baptizing of the newborn. If nothing much is at stake in infant baptism, why risk aggrieved hostility from disappointed parents and grandparents, and possibly their once-for-all alienation from Christianity, by trying to implement respectable baptismal discipline? Every infant baptism is an opportunity for evangelism or pre-evangelism, and as for the baptized child a contact has been established which may lead on to future conversion and personal profession of faith. But don't expect me, so our evangelical pastor tells himself or herself, to believe that this baptized baby is now a Christian or regenerate or even a member of the church, that is to say, that anything substantial is true of the child by virtue of baptism, and in particular any claim open to subsequent verification.

This chain of events and reasoning is, to be sure, not the only route which leads to low views of the sacrament of baptism. A certain anti-sacramentalism, or at least disinterest in the sacraments, has characterized too much evangelicalism, often as a reaction against an intolerably high sacramental theology, of the kind associated in the

Anglican tradition with the Tractarians' Oxford Movement or with Anglo-Catholicism in general. Liberalism in theological belief has often been accompanied by a distaste for the heavily liturgical or cultic expressions of church life, but by no means always. My observation of a mixed mainline Presbyterian church suggests that increasing lack of confidence among ministers in the truth of, say, the Apostles' Creed is not infrequently compensated for, so to speak, by a heightened concern for the sacraments. However we plot these often-complex currents of belief and unbelief, indifference and enthusiasm, there can, I judge, be no denying that many ministers have reached their minimizing convictions about baptism partly by way of reaction to others' perceived exaggerations. I have been present at repeated infant baptisms at which ministers have been at pains to tell us what the rite does not do or what does not happen in it, although I am grateful so far to have missed out on observances of the Lord's supper at which the person presiding says, in so many words, 'Nothing happens in this service.'

This is all a far cry from the New Testament. It is an instructive exercise simply to tabulate all of its varied references to and statements about baptism, and then to ask yourself whether this is an ordinance or sacrament which is merely symbolic rather than truly effective as a means by which Christ or the Holy Spirit works our blessing. Let me take you fairly quickly through many of these texts, conscious though I am that several of them could each justify an exegetical essay on its own.

On the birthday or re-birthday of the Christian church at Pentecost, Peter's reply to those among his hearers cut to the quick by his preaching and anxious to know how to move forward was 'Repent and be baptized, every one of you, in the name of Jesus Christ for the forgiveness of your sins' (Acts 2:38). I have heard a few sermons on this first Christian sermon but not one that stopped to comment on 'be baptized'. We should not separate repentance from baptism as what receives the forgiveness of sins, but then most of us would have replaced 'be baptized' with 'believe', and talked about baptism later. Even John Calvin claimed that Peter's order was not correct since in reality baptism does not precede but follows remission of sins as its seal.[2] Saul, soon to be Paul, was told by Ananias, 'Get up, be baptized and wash your sins away' (Acts 22:16). Other texts show that the baptismal waters spoke prominently of spiritual cleansing. Writing to the Corinthians and reminding them of the kinds of sinfulness some of them once practised, Paul declared, 'But you were washed, you were sanctified, you were justified in the name of Jesus Christ and by the Spirit of our God' (1 Cor. 6:11). It may well be that the whole of this affirmation is grounded in the baptism which washing in the name of Christ here denotes. Or again there is Paul (or some Paulinist) repeating to Titus that God our Saviour 'saved us through the washing of rebirth and renewal by the Holy Spirit, whom he poured out on us generously through Jesus Christ our Saviour' (Tit. 3:5–6). The baptismal interpretation of this verse is not beyond questioning, but 'washing' is an unexpected metaphor to use of rebirth if it is rejected.

The conjunction of washing, rebirth and the Spirit recalls one of the most influential of New Testament references to baptism, for so it has generally been taken, John 3:5, 'I tell you the truth, no one can enter the kingdom of God unless he is born of water and the Spirit.' This cursory review is no place to attempt to resolve

---

[2] *Calvin's Commentaries. The Acts of the Apostles 1–13* (trans. John W. Fraser and W.J.G. McDonald; Edinburgh: St Andrew Press, 1965), 79.

conclusively the meaning of this heavily contested text, but we should note that it was probably second to none in popularity among the post-apostolic generations on baptism. Finally, in a more enigmatic verse Peter declares that the water through which Noah and company were saved prefigured 'baptism that now saves you also – not the removal of dirt from the body but the pledge [or, response] of a good conscience toward God. It saves you by the resurrection of Jesus Christ' (1 Pet. 3:21). That is at its core a remarkably full-blooded assertion about baptism, and totally unambiguous, although the meaning of 'saves' has to be determined rather than assumed. In the longer ending of Mark's Gospel, 'Whoever believes and is baptized will be saved, but whoever does not believe will be condemned' (Mk. 16:16) has had a long innings and was freely cited by some of the Reformers in their earlier writings, but cannot be regarded as part of original Mark.

There is a further range of baptismal affirmations which have nothing to do with washing and cleansing from sin. Romans 6 links baptism and sin through the baptizand's identification with Christ in death, burial and resurrection (vv. 2–11). The candidate dies to sin and rises to new life and thereby is freed from sin. Thus through baptism it is more the grip or power of sin that is overcome than its guilt and uncleanness. Colossians 2:11–12, which likens Christ's death to his circumcision, conveys a message similar to Romans 6:

> In him also you were circumcised with a spiritual circumcision, by putting off the body of the flesh in the circumcision of Christ; when you were buried with him in baptism, you were also raised with him through faith in the power of God, who raised him from the dead.[3]

---

[3] NRSV translation.

Romans 6:6 speaks of our old self being crucified, while in Colossians 2:11 it is the body of the flesh which is put off. Later in Colossians, in a context almost certainly baptismal in its associations, the readers are declared to have stripped off the old self and clothed themselves with the new self (Col. 3:9–10). This is parallel to Galatians 3:27, 'all of you who were baptized into Christ have clothed yourselves with [have put on] Christ.'

There are yet other divine works or gifts focussed on baptism, including the receiving of the Holy Spirit. Earlier in this lecture I cut my quotation of Acts 2 short at the first part of verse 38; the rest goes on, 'And you will receive the gift of the Holy Spirit.' The disciples at Ephesus who had received only John's baptism were baptized by Paul 'into the name of the Lord Jesus' and received the Holy Spirit when he laid hands on them (Acts 19:5–6). Cornelius and his family and friends were baptized because they had received the Spirit already (Acts 10:47–48). No tidy schema can be constructed out of these divergent experiences in Acts, but the bond between baptism and the receiving of the Spirit remains clear throughout.

I have cut many an exegetical corner but I am not assuming the mantle of a biblical commentator. My concern has been simply to convey a sense of the markedly direct terms in which the New Testament documents attribute the multifaceted reception of God's salvation to the instrumentality of baptism. This is what I mean by the strongly realist presentation of baptism in the New Testament. There is not a single text which prima facie ascribes to baptism only a symbolical or representational or significatory function. My argument depends, as I well realize, on the Greek verb and noun denoting the rite of baptism itself, which would not in every instance command universal consent. Some would interpret being 'baptized with Christ Jesus' in Romans 6:3 not of being immersed or soaked in the baptismal water but of a spiritual experience of which water baptism is a sign or symbol. I think that this reading blunts the force of Paul's expostulation with certain misguided Christians because it places at one remove the hard fact of water baptism which they had all gone through. Others deal similarly with 1 Corinthians 12:13, which I have not yet cited in this discussion:

> we were all baptized by one Spirit into one body – whether Jews or Greeks, slaves or free – and we were all given the one Spirit to drink.

What clinches a literal reference here for me is the parenthesis, 'whether Jews or Greeks, slaves or free', which as we confidently gather from Galatians 3:27–28 and most probably Colossians 3:9–11 was a primitive affirmation of baptism. In the first lecture we touched on the prominent unifying role of baptism in the apostolic churches; 'there is one Lord, one faith, one baptism' (Eph. 4:5). The unusual language of drinking the Spirit in 1 Corinthians 12:13 harks back to the beginning of chapter 10, where Paul portrays the blessings of the Israelites of the Exodus in terms of the new covenant sacraments. Their having been 'baptized into Moses in the cloud and in the sea' may be, on my reading of the documents, the sole non-literal use of baptism language in the New Testament after the Gospels, yet the physical elements of cloud and sea show that this is not a spiritualized usage but rather a transference of baptism proper to another watery experience, of solidarity with Moses.

But I can well understand preachers in churches which practise baby baptism and hardly ever have a baptism of a believer finding a spiritualizing interpretation of Romans

6 and 1 Corinthians 12:13 much more congenial. As I have emphasized more than once before now, the long reign of infant baptism has made the New Testament's portrayal of baptism almost alien. The remoteness is enhanced by the problematic realism of the apostolic writers' baptismal language. What in a sense creates the difficulty is the often unspoken assumption that there is but one baptism, that the baptism given to infants is the same baptism given to Cornelius and company. Apologetic for infant baptism generally aims to demonstrate that infants are proper recipients of the one Christian baptism of Acts and the Epistles, not that there is a distinct and special baptism intended for babies alone. This assumption, which is surely completely sound, throws up dilemmas when it feels awkward to describe infant baptism in the language of Romans 6, Galatians 3, Colossians 2 and 1 Corinthians 12 – and thereupon spiritualizing exegesis comes into favour.

If one has coped with the uncomfortable baptismal realism of the New Testament, it is presumably a lesser challenge to repeat the task with the creeds and confessions of the churches. The only ecumenical creed to mention baptism is the Nicene (none mentions the eucharist) in the phrase 'one baptism for the remission of sins'. I have argued elsewhere that this cannot have originally embraced babies, because in the circles from which this creed emerged, to be approved at the Council of Constantinople in 381 (if we accept the testimony of the Fathers at the Council of Chalcedon seventy years later, as most scholars do), it was believed that newborn babies had no sins.[4] John Chrysostom once said:

---

[4] D.F. Wright, 'The Meaning and Reference of "One Baptism for the Remission of Sins" in the Niceno-Constantinopolitan Creed', in *Studia Patristica* XIX (1989), 281–85.

> Although many people think that the only gift [baptism] confers is the remission of sins, we have counted its honors to the number of ten. It is on this account that we baptize even infants, although they have no sins.[5]

Nevertheless things were different in the West, where a generation after the council of 381 AD Augustine's theology would begin its lengthy domination of baptismal thinking. Baptism became the sole means of deliverance from the guilt of original sin and of receiving eternal life. The saving significance of this essentially effective baptism came during the middles ages to be attended by increasing superstitions. The Reformers were all Augustinian in theology – the whole Reformation was an Augustinian movement – so that, although they stripped infant baptism of impure accretions and did not in the main endorse the necessity of infant baptism for salvation, they did not empty the rite of its efficacy.

Our survey of Reformation confessions and similar official formulations begins with that moderate Reformation in England. Number 27 of the 39 Articles (1562) states that baptism is not only a visible differentiation between Christians and others but also

> a sign of Regeneration or New-Birth, whereby, as by an instrument, they that receive Baptism rightly are grafted into the Church; the promises of the forgiveness of sin, and of our adoption to be the sons of God by the Holy Ghost, are visibly signed and sealed; Faith is confirmed, and Grace increased by virtue of prayer unto God.[6]

---

[5] John Chrysostom, *Homily 3 to the Neophytes* 6, in *St. John Chrysostom: Baptismal Instructions* (trans. Paul W. Harkins; Ancient Christian Writers 31; New York and Ramsey, NJ: Newman Press, 1963), 57, here adapted.

[6] The 39 Articles appear in all printings of the 1662 *Book of Common Prayer* (but not *Common Worship*, 2000), and often elsewhere, e.g. in

This may seem finely balanced between the language of instrumentality and that of signification and sealing. If we allow the 1552 *Book of Common Prayer* to interpret the article for us, it has this prayer before the baptism:

> Geue thy holy spirite to these infantes, that they maye bee borne agayne, and bee made heyres of euerlastinge saluacion,[7]

and after the baptism declares: 'Seeyng nowe ... that these children be regenerate and grafted into the bodye of Christes congregacion ...'[8] The Scots Confession of 1560 'utterly condemn(s)' the emptiness of viewing the sacraments as merely 'naked and bare signs', and continues:

> [W]e assuredly believe that by Baptism we are engrafted into Christ Jesus, to be made partakers of His righteousness, by which our sins are covered and remitted.[9]

The order of baptism in the first Reformed *Book of Common Order* (1564) opens with this question to the child's father and godfather:

> Do you present this childe to be baptised, earnestly desiring that he may be ingrafted in the mysticall body of Jesus Christ?[10]

The long exposition and exhortation put into the mouth of a minister in this service leaves no doubt that 'the justice [righteousness] of Jesus Christ is made ours by baptisme',

---

[6] *(continued)* Leith (ed.), *Creeds of the Churches*, 275–76.
[7] *The First and Second Prayer-Books of King Edward the Sixth*, 396.
[8] Ibid., 398.
[9] Scots Confession 21, in Arthur C. Cochrane (ed.), *Reformed Confessions of the 16th Century* (London: SCM Press, 1966), 179.
[10] *The Liturgy of John Knox* (Glasgow: University Press, 1886), 153.

that 'we are clad in Baptisme' in 'purenes and perfection', that, just as water washes off external filth, so inwardly the virtue of Christ's blood purges our souls from corruption, and that in baptism children are received into the bosom of Christ's congregation.[11] A temporal qualification is included in the assertion that

> our Saviour Christ, who commanded baptisme to be ministred, will, by the power of his Holy Spirite, effectually worke in the harts of his elect (in tyme convenient) all that is ment and signified by the same. And this the Scripture calleth our regeneration.[12]

If we turn to the Lutheran world, Luther's Small Catechism gives this answer to the question 'What gifts or benefits does Baptism bestow?'

> It effects forgiveness of sins, delivers from death and the devil, and grants eternal salvation to all who believe.[13]

Luther cites Mark 16:16, Titus 3:5–8 and Romans 6:4.[14] In the more diffuse article on baptism in his Large Catechism, according to the two divine words on which it is founded, Matthew 28:19 and Mark 16:16, 'it is solemnly and strictly commanded that we must be baptized or we shall not be saved'.[15] Later the article affirms:

> To put it most simply, the power, effect, benefit, fruit and purpose of Baptism is to save ... To be saved, we know is nothing

---

[11] Ibid., 155–56.
[12] Ibid., 155.
[13] Luther, *Small Catechism* 4:5–6, in *The Book of Concord: The Confessions of the Evangelical Lutheran Church* (trans. and ed. Theodore G. Tappert; Philadelphia: Fortress Press, 1959), 348–49.
[14] Luther, *Small Catechism* 4:8, 10, 14, in *The Book of Concord*, 349.
[15] Luther, *Large Catechism* 4:3–5, 6, in *The Book of Concord*, 437.

else than to be delivered from sin, death, and the devil and to enter into the kingdom of Christ and live with him forever.[16]

Reformed confessions characteristically display a less forthright approach to the sacraments than the Lutheran, yet still announce a confidence in the gifts of baptism. The Belgic Confession of 1561, still highly respected among Dutch Reformed churches, says this:

> [T]he Ministers, on their part, administer the sacrament, and that which is visible, but our Lord giveth that which is signified by the Sacrament, namely, the gifts and invisible grace; washing, cleansing, and purging our souls of all filth and unrighteousness; renewing our hearts and filling them with all comfort; giving unto us a true assurance of his fatherly goodness; putting on us the new man, and putting off the old man with all his deeds.[17]

Noteworthy in this and similar articles is the use of the verb 'signify' of the relation between the external and human and the internal and divine aspects of baptism itself, not in terms of baptism signifying something that happens through other means at another time. So the Confession of the English-speaking congregation in Geneva (1556), which was printed in early editions of the Scottish *Form of Prayers* or *Book of Common Order*, has this brief statement only:

> [A]s by baptism once received is signified that we (infants as well as others of age and discretion) being strangers from God by original sin, are received into His family and congregation, with full assurance that although this root

---

[16] Luther, *Large Catechism* 4:24–25, in *The Book of Concord*, 439.
[17] Belgic Confession 34; Cochrane (ed.), *Reformed Confessions*, 214.

of sin lies hidden in us, yet to the elect it shall not be imputed.[18]

Widely respected as the most mature of the Reformed confessions is the Second Helvetic (Swiss) Confession of 1566, the work of Heinrich Bullinger. Here is part of its article on baptism:

> Now to be baptized in the name of Christ is to be enrolled, entered, and received into the covenant and family, and so into the inheritance of the sons of God ... to be cleansed also from the filthiness of sins, and to be granted the manifold grace of God, in order to lead a new and innocent life.[19]

After enumerating God's mercies and gifts of grace the text continues:

> All these things are assured by baptism. For inwardly we are regenerated, purified, and renewed by God through the Holy Spirit; and outwardly we receive the assurance of the greatest gifts in the water, by which also those great benefits are represented, and, as it were, set before our eyes to be beheld.[20]

Finally, a later but highly influential document, the Westminster Confession of Faith of 1647. Listen to these two paragraphs which make strong affirmations along with standard qualifications:

> Although it be a great sin to contemn or neglect this ordinance [of baptism], yet grace and salvation are not so

---

[18] Confession of Faith of the English Congregation at Geneva 4; Cochrane (ed.), *Reformed Confessions*, 134–5.
[19] Second Helvetic Confession 20; Cochrane (ed.), *Reformed Confessions*, 282.
[20] Ibid.

inseparably annexed unto it, as that no person can be regenerated or saved without it, or that all that are baptized are undoubtedly regenerated.

The efficacy of baptism is not tied to that moment of time wherein it is administered; yet notwithstanding, by the right use of this ordinance, the grace promised is not only offered, but really exhibited and conferred by the Holy Ghost, to such (whether of age or infants) as that grace belongeth unto, according to the counsel of God's own will, in his appointed time.[21]

The reservation, that God has not so bound his working to the sacrament as to be unable to work without it and that not all the baptized are of the elect, cannot disguise the fact that the Westminster Confession teaches baptismal regeneration of infants and older persons.[22] Just as these qualifications are commonplace among the Reformers, so also the generality of their baptismal theology conveys a decisively realist message: baptism is God's normal channel for imparting his gifts – which are variously enumerated – to his children.

This consensus addresses a challenge to present-day heirs of the Reformation, who on the whole have not succeeded in remaining faithful to its baptismal realism. Evangelical Anglicans have not been of one mind in the face of the widespread disuse of the 1662 Prayer Book in favour of recent alternatives such as *Common Worship* (2000), but most must be glad not to have to repeat with 1662 that 'this Child is by Baptism regenerate'. Baptism is often given a future reference, so that infants are said to be

---

[21] Westminster Confession of Faith 28:5, 6, in Leith (ed.), *Creeds of the Churches*, 224–25. The verb 'exhibited' and its Latin original, *exhibere*, were widely used in Reformed eucharistic discussion in the Reformation era in the sense not so much of 'display' but of 'bestow, confer'.

[22] Cf. my essay 'Baptism at the Westminster Assembly'.

baptized into future faith and repentance or to be designated for a life of salvation. Such notes are indeed found in Calvin also, but then Calvin believed that infants were baptized because they were already regenerate. Too much anxiety has been expended on whether baptism makes a person a Christian. The word 'Christian' itself scarcely gets defined in the New Testament, where it may bear no more than a conventional reference to the followers of Jesus Christ in a social or communal sense.

Such modern evangelical unease with the efficacy of baptism is not fully intelligible without taking cognizance of what 'the long reign of infant baptism' has done to it. There have been calls for a moratorium on the administration of paedobaptism among American Methodists and even Catholics. In the sixteenth century some of the leading Reformers went through phases of extreme frustration at trying to promote a godly faithful church on the basis of universal infant baptism. Some of them resorted for a time to working with small groups of true believers pledged to a committed evangelical devotion and discipline incapable of being expected from the whole population.[23]

Still today within mixed denominations tensions continue between different baptismal policies. Some, often the more evangelical, favour a stricter administration, only for the children of regularly attending and active church members. They might regard their own church's regulations as too lax. Others would prefer never to turn anyone away, and may baptize children whose parents have been refused by a neighbouring minister. Despite the significant renewal of baptismal belief evident among both paedobaptist and believers' baptist communions, the

---

[23] Cf. David F. Wright, 'Sixteenth-Century Reformed Perspectives on the Minority Church', in John H. Leith (ed.), *Calvin Studies VII* (Davidson College, NC, 1994), 15–29; reprinted in *Scottish Journal of Theology* 48 (1995), 469–88.

decline of the churches in the West moves some to embrace unquestioningly anyone who shows the slightest interest in the church. In such a context baptism, especially of infants, may be turned to all kinds of other uses, as a rite of babyhood, the religious icing on the cake of a family get-together, an expression of the church's goodwill towards the more-or-less unchurched community, at its best perhaps an affirmation of God's love for everybody, an evangelistic toehold in another house in the parish, to encourage parents towards responsible childcare, to show solidarity with a single parent, to avoid offending grandparents of a child who may themselves, unlike the parents, be active in the congregation, a general-purpose social cement.

During 1997–99 the Church of Scotland's Committee on Mission and Evangelism Resources conducted a far-reaching survey of views and attitudes towards infant baptism as practised in its parishes. Among the focus groups whose opinions it canvassed were four, in different kinds of social settings, representing the periphery of the Church – mostly people who called themselves Christians but rarely if ever attended church. A very clear majority of them (32 out of 40) believed that anyone who wanted to should be able to have their baby baptized. Just over half (twenty-one) held that baptism had an effect on the child, while thirteen denied this. But when asked if a baptized baby was more likely to go to church when older, all forty said no, and 32 out of 40 said the same about the parents of the baby baptized.[24] The juxtaposition of these two strong opinions – demanding baptism for any who wanted, and denying it had any bearing on later church attendance –

---

[24] The Committee's report on 'Infant Baptism and Mission and Evangelism in the Church of Scotland: 1963–1997' is found in *Reports of the General Assembly of the Church of Scotland 1999* (Edinburgh: St Andrew

starkly illustrates what 'the long reign of infant baptism' has done to baptism.

Baptism, Eucharist and Ministry (1982) urged efforts be made to put a stop to indiscriminate infant baptism.[25] While recognizing that forceful social trends, or rather ministers' and congregations' responses to them, weigh in the scales against this plea, the time is ripe for a recovery of the New Testament integrity of baptism, including infant baptism. Because fewer requests for baby baptism are now being made, in many local situations a responsible baptismal discipline is more feasible. It should both facilitate and be facilitated by a recovery of a more biblically realist understanding of baptism with which Christ furnished his church to mark incorporation into him and his body.[26]

---

[24] *(continued)* Press, 1999), 20/67–20/92. The details given above are taken from an unpublished 'draft full version' of the Committee's report, more extensive than the published report, at 6–7.

[25] Cf. *Baptism, Eucharist and Ministry*, 7 (Baptism: Commentary 21): 'In many large European and North American majority churches infant baptism is often practised in an apparently indiscriminate way. This contributes to the reluctance of churches which practise believers' baptism to acknowledge the validity of infant baptism; this fact should lead to more critical reflection on the meaning of baptism within those majority churches themselves.'

[26] For supporting argument from a Reformed base see Rich Lusk, 'Paedobaptism and Baptismal Efficacy: Historic Trends and Current Controversies', in Steve Wilkins and Duane Garner (eds), *The Federal Vision* (Monroe, LA: Athanasius Press, 2004), 71–125.

Bibliography

The Alternative Service Book 1980 (Oxford: Oxford University Press, 1984)

Armour, Rollin Stely, *Anabaptist Baptism: A Representative Study* (Studies in Anabaptist and Mennonite History 11; Scottdale, PA: Herald Press, 1966)

Baptism, Eucharist and Ministry (Faith and Order Paper 111; Geneva: World Council of Churches, 1982),

Barth, K., *The Teaching of the Church Regarding Baptism* (trans. E.A. Payne; London: SCM Press, 1948)

—, *Church Dogmatics*, Vol. IV/4 (trans. G.W. Bromiley; Edinburgh: T&T Clark, 1969)

Beasley-Murray, G.R., *Baptism Today and Tomorrow* (London: MacMillan, 1966)

Becoming a Christian: The Ecumenical Implications of our Common Baptism (report of a Faith and Order Consultation held at Faverges, France, 17–24 January 1997)

Book of Common Order 1928 (London: Oxford University Press, 1928)

Book of Common Order of the Church of Scotland (London: Oxford University Press, 1940)

Book of Common Order of the Church of Scotland (Edinburgh: St Andrew Press, 1994)

Bradshaw, P.F., M.E. Johnson and L.E. Phillips, *The Apostolic Tradition. A Commentary* (Hermeneia; Minneapolis, MN: Fortress Press, 2002)

Calvin, John, *Calvin's Commentaries. The Acts of the Apostles 1–13* (trans. J.W. Fraser and W.J.G. McDonald; Edinburgh: St Andrew Press, 1965)

Cameron, Nigel M. de S., D.F. Wright et al. (eds.), *Dictionary of Scottish Church History and Theology* (Edinburgh: T&T Clark, 1993)

Catechism of the Catholic Church (London: Geoffrey Chapman, 1994)

Chrysostom, John, *Baptismal Instructions* (trans. P.W. Harkins; Ancient Christian Writers 31; New York and Ramsey, NJ: Newman Press, 1963)

Church of the Nazarene, *Manual 2001–2005* (Kansas City, MO: Nazarene Publishing House, 2002)

Cochrane, A.C. (ed.), *Reformed Confessions of the 16th Century* (London: SCM Press, 1966)

Common Worship. Services and Prayers for the Church of England (London: Church House Publishing, 2000)

Cramer, P., *Baptism and Change in the Early Middle Ages c. 200 – c. 1150* (Cambridge: Cambridge University Press, 1993)

Cressy, D., *Birth, Marriage, and Death. Ritual, Religion, and the Life-Cycle in Tudor and Stuart England* (Oxford: Oxford University Press, 1997)

Cross, A.R., *Baptism and the Baptists. Theology and Practice in Twentieth-Century Britain* (Carlisle: Paternoster Press, 2000)

Cross, A.R. and P.E. Thompson, *Baptist Sacramentalism* (Studies in Baptist History and Thought 5; Carlisle: Paternoster Press, 2003)

Cullmann, O., *Baptism in the New Testament* (trans. J.K.S. Reid; Studies in Biblical Theology 1; London: SCM Press, 1950)

—, 'The Tradition', in his *The Early Church* (trans. and ed. A.J.B. Higgins; London: SCM Press, 1956), 55–99

Cuming, G.J., *Hippolytus: A Text for Students* (Grove Liturgical Study 8; Bramcote, Notts: Grove Books, 1976)

De Latte, R., 'Saint Augustin et le baptême: Étude liturgico-historique du ritual baptismal des enfants chez S. Augustin', *Questions liturgiques* 57 (1976), 41–55

Didier, J.C., 'Une adaptation de la liturgie baptismale au baptême des enfants dans l'Église ancienne', *Mélanges de science religieuse* 22 (1965), 79–90

Ferguson, E., 'Inscriptions and the Origins of Infant Baptism', *Journal of Theological Studies* 30 (1979), 37–46, Reprinted in E. Ferguson (ed.), *Studies in Early Christianity*, Vol. 11: *Conversion, Catechumenate and Baptism in the Early Church* (18 Vols; New York: Garland Publishing, 1993), 391–400

The First and Second Prayer-Books of King Edward the Sixth (Everyman's Library; London: J.M. Dent & Sons, New York: E.P. Dutton & Co., n.d.)

Fisher, J.D.C., *Christian Initiation: Baptism in the Medieval West* (Alcuin Club Collections 47; London: SPCK, 1965)

—, *Christian Initiation: The Reformation Period* (Alcuin Club Collections 51; London: SPCK, 1970)

Flemington, W.F., *The New Testament Doctrine of Baptism* (London: SPCK, 1957)

Ford, J., *In the Steps of John Wesley: The Church of the Nazarene in Britain* (Kansas City, MO: Nazarene Publishing House, 1968)

Panel on Doctrine Report, 'Baptism', in *General Assembly 2003* (Edinburgh: Church of Scotland Board of Practice and Procedure, 2003), 13/1–13/17

Hawthorne, G.F. and R.P. Martin (eds.), *Dictionary of Paul and his Letters* (Downers Grove, IL/Leicester: InterVarsity Press, 1993)

Hobhouse, W., *The Church and the World in Idea and History* (Bampton Lectures 1909; London: MacMillan & Co., 1911^2)

Hombert, P.-M., *Nouvelles recherches de chronologie Augustinienne* (Collection des Études Augustiniennes, Sér. Antiq. 163; Paris: Institut d' Études Augustiniennes, 2000)

'Infant Baptism and Mission and Evangelism in the Church of Scotland: 1963–1997', in *Reports of the General Assembly of the Church of Scotland 1999* (Edinburgh: St Andrew Press, 1999), 20/67–20/92

Isidore, *De ecclesiasticis officiis*, in *Corpus Christianorum* 113 (ed. C.M. Lawson; Turnhout: Brepols, 1989)

Jeremias, J., *Infant Baptism in the First Four Centuries* (trans. David Cairns; London: SCM Press, 1960

Johnson, M.E., 'Scrutinies, Baptismal' in P. Bradshaw (ed.), *The New SCM Dictionary of Liturgy and Worship* (London: SCM Press, 2002), 427

Johnson, M.E., *The Rites of Christian Initiation: Their Evolution and Interpretation* (Collegeville, MN: Liturgical Press, 1999)

Johnsson, L., *Baptist Reconsideration of Baptism and Ecclesiology* (European University Studies XXIII: 716; Frankfurt am Main: Peter Lang, 2000)

Keefe, S.A., *Water and the Word: Baptism and the Education of the Clergy in the Carolingian Empire*, Vol. 2 (2 Vols; Notre Dame, IN: University of Notre Dame Press, 2002)

Kennedy, J., *The Days of the Fathers in Ross-shire* (enlarged edn.; Inverness: 'Northern Chronicle' Office, 1897)

Kinzig, W., *In Search of Asterius. Studies on the Authorship of the Homilies on the Psalms* (Göttingen: Vandenhoeck & Ruprecht, 1990)

Kreider, A., *Worship and Evangelism in Pre-Christendom* (Alcuin/ GROW Joint Liturgical Studies 32; Cambridge: Grove Books, 1995)

Leith, J.H. (ed.), *Creeds of the Churches* (Richmond, VA: John Knox Press, 1973^2)

Leithart, P., 'Infant Baptism in History: An Unfinished Tragicomedy', in Gregg Strawbridge (ed.), *The Case for Covenantal Infant Baptism* (Phillipsburg, NJ: P&R Publishing, 2003) 246–62

Liturgy of John Knox, The (Glasgow: University Press, 1886)

Lusk, Rich, 'Paedobaptism and Baptismal Efficacy: Historic Tremds and Current Controversies' in Steve Wilkins and Duane Garner (eds.), *The Federal Vision* (Monroe, LA: Athanasius Press, 2004), 71–125

Luther, M., *Small Catechism*, in *The Book of Concord: The Confessions of the Evangelical Lutheran Church* (trans. and ed. Theodore G. Tappert; Philadelphia: Fortress Press, 1959)

Manning, B. Lord, *Why Not Abandon the Church?* (London: Independent Press, 1939)

Martin, R.P. and P.H. Davids (eds.), *Dictionary of the Later New Testament & Its Developments* (Downers Grove, IL/Leicester: InterVarsity Press, 1997), 255–60

Mayer, C. (ed.), *Augustinus-Lexikon*, Vol. 1 (Basel: Schwabe & Co. AG, 1986–94)

Rite of Christian Initiation of Adults (study edn; Chicago: Liturgy Training Publications, 1988)

The Rites of the Catholic Church, Vol. 1 (Collegeville, MN: Liturgical Press, 1990)

Stark, R., *The Rise of Christianity* (Princeton, NJ: Princeton University Press, 1996)

Strauss, G., *Luther's House of Learning. Indoctrination of the Young in the German Reformation* (Baltimore: Johns Hopkins University Press, 1978)

Tertullian, *Apology*.

—, *Tertullian's Homily on Baptism* (trans. Ernest Evans; London: SPCK, 1964)

Vatican Council II, 'Constitution on the Sacred Liturgy (*Sacrosanctum concilium*)' in *Vatican Council II: The Conciliar and Post Conciliar Documents* (trans A. Flannery; Collegeville, MN: Liturgical Press, 1980^2)

Whitaker, E.C., *Documents of the Baptismal Liturgy* (3rd edn.; ed. Maxwell E. Johnson; Alcuin Club Collections 79; London: SPCK, 2003)

Willimon, W.H., *Peculiar Speech: Preaching to the Baptized* (Grand Rapids, MI: Eerdmans, 1992)

Willis, G.G., *Saint Augustine and the Donatist Controversy* (London: SPCK, 1950)

Wright, David F., 'Donatist Theologoumena in Augustine? Baptism, Reviviscence of Sins and Unworthy Ministers', in *Congresso Internazionale su S. Agostino … Atti II* (Rome: Institutum Patristicum Augustinianum, 1987), 213–24

—, 'The Origins of Infant Baptism – Child Believers' Baptism?', *Scottish Journal of Theology* 40 (1987), 1–23

—, 'The Meaning and Reference of "One Baptism for the Remission of Sins" in the Niceno-Constantinopolitan Creed', *Studia Patristica* XIX (1989), 281–85

—, 'Sixteenth-Century Reformed Perspectives on the Minority Church', in J.H. Leith (ed.), *Calvin Studies VII* (Davidson College, NC, 1994), 15–29. Reprinted in *Scottish Journal of Theology* 48 (1995), 469–88

—, 'Baptism at the Westminster Assembly', in J.H. Leith (ed.), *The Westminster Confession in Current Thought* (Calvin Studies VIII; Davidson College, NC, 1996), 76–90. Reprinted in J. Ligon Duncan (ed.), *The Westminster Confession into the 21st Century*, Vol. 1 (Fearn, Ross-shire: Christian Focus Publications, 2003), 161–85

—, 'Infant Dedication in the Early Church', in S.E. Porter and A.R. Cross (eds.), *Baptism, the New Testament and the Church. Historical and Contemporary Studies in Honour of R.E.O. White* (Journal for the Study of the New Testament, Suppl. Ser. 171; Sheffield: Sheffield Academic Press, 1999), 352–78

—, 'Habitats of Infant Baptism', in W.M. Alston, Jr. (ed.), *Theology in the Service of the Church. Essays in Honor of Thomas W. Gillespie* (Grand Rapids, MI: Eerdmans, 2000), 254–65

—, 'Augustine and the Transformation of Baptism', in A. Kreider (ed.), *The Origins of Christendom in the West* (Edinburgh, New York: T&T Clark, 2001), 287–310

—, 'Out, In, Out: Jesus' Blessing of the Children and Infant Baptism', in S.E. Porter and A.R. Cross (eds.), *Dimensions of Baptism. Biblical and Theological Studies* (Journal for the Study of the New Testament Suppl. Ser. 234; London, New York: Sheffield Academic Press, 2002), 188–206

—, 'A Family Faith: Domestic Discipling', in *Bibliotheca Sacra* 160 (2003), 259–68

Biblical Index

Ezekiel
1:10   48

Matthew
5:42   75
19:13–15   70, 72
19:14   75
28:19   96

Mark
7:31–35   70
10:13–16   23, 73
16:16   90, 96

Luke
14:23   20

John
3:5   75, 89–90

Acts   63
2:38   89, 91
10:47–48   91
16:15   36
16:31–34   36
19:5–6   91
22:16   89

Romans
6   61, 92–93
6:2–11   90
6:3   91–92
6:3–4   33
6:3–14   76
6:4   96
6:6   91
10:14, 17   53

1 Corinthians
1:13   32
6:11   89
10:1–2   76, 92
12:12–13   32
12:13   76, 92, 93

Galatians
3:26–28   32, 93
3:27   76, 91
3:27–28   92

Ephesians
4:5   31, 92

Colossians
2:11–12   90–91, 93
3:9   76
3:9–10   91
3:9–11   92
3:11   32
3:12   76

Titus
3:5 76
3:5–6 89
3:5–8 96

1 Peter
3:21 90

1 John
4:19 22

Index of Modern Authors

Alston, Jr, Wallace M. 82
Armour, Rollin Stely 29–30

Barth, Karl 13, 17, 77
Beasley-Murray, George R. 5
Bradshaw, Paul 38–39, 40, 63, 64, 66, 71–72
Brown, Peter 25

Cameron, Nigel M. de S. 18
Cochrane, Arthur C. 95, 97, 98
Corblet, Jules 1
Cramer, Peter 2, 8, 20
Cressy, David 27
Cross, Anthony R. 28, 43, 72
Cullmann, Oscar 18, 31
Cuming, Geoffrey J. 39

Davids, Peter H. 38
De Latte, R. 42
Didier, J.C. 42
Duncan, III, J. Ligon 24

Evans, Ernest 75

Ferguson, Everett 37
Fisher, J.D.C. 27, 46, 54–57, 68, 69–70, 73
Flannery, Austin 78
Flemington, W.F. 21–22

Ford, Jack 16
Fraser, John W. 89

Garner, Duane 102

Harkins, Paul W. 94
Hawthorne, Gerald F. 38
Hobhouse, Walter 74
Höflung, Johann Wilhelm Friedrich 2
Hombert, Pierre-Marie 51

Jeremias, Joachim 3, 18, 42
Johnson, Maxwell E. 1, 25, 39, 47, 71–72, 78, 79, 80, 81, 82
Johnsson, Lennart 28
Jordahn, Bruno 1

Keefe, Susan A. 49–53
Keith, Graham 4
Kennedy, John 4
Kinzig, Wolfram 42
Kreider, Alan 2, 60, 65
Kretschmar, Georg 1

Lamirande, Emilien 36
Lane, Tony vii–viii
Lawson, C.M. 53
Leith, John H. 4, 24, 95, 99, 100

Leithart, Peter 6, 7, 8
Lusk, Rich 102

McDonald, W.J.G. 89
Manning, Bernard Lord 21
Martin, Ralph P. 38
Mayer, Cornelius 36
Moule, C.F.D. 18
Müller, K.F. 2

Noble, Tom ix, 16

Philip, James 21
Phillips, L. Edward 39
Porter, Stanley E. 43, 72

Stark, Rodney 67–68
Strauss, Gerald 69
Strawbridge, Gregg 6

Tappert, Theodore G. 96–97
Thompson, Philip E. 28
Torrance, T.F. 18

Wall, William 2
Whitaker, E.C. 47
Wilkins, Steve 102
Willimon, William H. 65
Willis, Geoffrey Grimshaw 26
Wright, David F. 6, 17, 18, 20, 24, 26, 38, 43, 50, 53, 67–68, 72, 82, 93, 99, 100

General Index

Admission to communion   23
Alpha course   65, 79
Alternative Service Book   15, 57–58, 59
Amalarius   50–51
Anabaptism, Anabaptists   4, 5, 11, 17, 19, 20
Anglicanism   4, 10, 12, 14
    see also Church of England
Anglo-Catholicism   88
Apostolic Tradition
    see Hippolytus
Asterius   41–43, 53
Augustine   6, 7, 12, 20, 25, 26, 36, 40, 41–43, 53, 64, 94
    Letter 98   50–51
    Baptism   53
    Confessions   64

baptism
    as ordination   32–33
    by heretics   26, 52
    by laity   25–27
    clinical, emergency   17, 25
    dual practice   viii, 11, 16, 17
    efficacy of   viii, 83–102
    household   3, 15, 36
    in blood   29, 64
    liturgy of   8, 9, 39–62, 72–73

    of infants
        (paedobaptism)   *passim*
    of believers (adults, converts)   *passim*
    questions and responses   8, 9, 40–46, 48–49, 95–96
    realist view of   88, 91–93, 99, 102
    symbolic view of   viii, 83–102
Baptism, Eucharist and Ministry
    (*BEM*)   10, 14, 15, 16, 36, 38, 102
Baptists   vii–viii, 5, 6, 8, 11, 16, 17, 28, 30–31, 33, 35
Barth, Karl   13, 17, 77
Belgic Confession   97
believers (*fidelis, pistos*)   36–37
Bible
    New Testament   viii, 5, 7, 14, 15, 16, 21, 22, 23, 31–33, 36,   37–38, 75–76, 81, 88–93, 102
    Old Testament   15
Blessing of children
    (Mk. 10:13–16, par.)   23–24, 70, 72–74
blood-baptism   64
Boniface   50–51

Book of Common Order
  1564 19, 55–56, 82, 95–96, 97
  1928 59
  1940 59–60
  1994 22, 60–61, 62, 81, 82, 84
Book of Common Prayer 23
  1549 19, 23, 45, 46, 54, 73
  1552 19, 45, 73, 95
  1559 19
  1662 19, 35, 43–45, 58, 99
Brandenburg-Nuremberg Church Order 54
Bucer, Martin 45, 54–55, 73
Bullinger, Heinrich 98

Calvin, John 19–20, 89
catechisms 68, 69
Catechism of the Catholic Church 15
catechumen 36, 63, 69–72
catechumenate 46, 62, 63–82
Chalcedon, council of 93
Charlemagne 49
children's ministries 67
Christendom vii–viii, 9, 11–33, 74, 86
church 84–86
  as baptismal community 31–32, 36
  membership 83–86
church-door ceremony 69–73
Church of England 8, 9, 13, 15, 23, 43–46, 56, 57–59, 86, 88
  see also *Alternative Service Book, Book of Common Prayer, Common Worship*
Church of Scotland 14, 18, 21, 23, 59–61, 62, 84–86, 101–102
  see also *Book of Common Order*
circumcision 15, 90

Commandments, Ten
  see Decalogue
Common Worship 8, 15, 58–59, 99
confessions of faith
  see Belgic, Geneva, Scots, Second Helvetic, Westminster
confirmation 23
Constantine 12, 63
Constantinople, council of 93, 94
councils of church
  see Chalcedon, Constantinople, Lateran, Nicaea, Vatican
covenant 16, 30
Cranmer, Thomas 73
Creeds 40–41
  Apostles' 40, 44, 48–49, 55, 56, 57, 59, 60–61, 62, 68, 88
  Nicene 93

Decalogue 68, 69
dedication of infants 43
discipleship 63–82
Donatism 53
Dutch Reformed churches 97

Easter 8, 48, 64, 69, 70, 76–77, 85
  see also Pascha
England 13
Ephphatha (Effeta) 70
eucharist
  see Lord's supper
Europe 12, 13, 49
Evangelical Covenant Church 16
evangelicals, evangelicalism 23, 24, 25, 33, 37, 87

exorcism   8, 48, 65

faith, profession of   4, 23, 35–62
   see also baptism of believers
Faith and Order   10, 14, 61–62
Fathers, early church   3, 6, 7, 9, 51–53, 63, 66, 72, 75–77
fidelis
   see believers
font   73
Form of Prayers   97
   see also Book of Common Order 1564
Forme des Prieres   55
French Reformed Church   16, 22
French Revolution   13

Gelasian Sacramentary   48, 71–72
Geneva   12, 16, 55, 97–98
   Confession of English Congregation   97–98
godparents
   see sponsors

Hippolytus, *Apostolic Tradition*   34–41, 64–67, 78
Holy Roman Empire   49

Ignatius Loyola, *Spiritual Exercises*   65
infants, baptism of   *passim*
initiation   86–87
inscriptions   37
Isidore   53

Jerome   40
John Chrysostom   7, 93–94
John the Deacon   47–48

Keswick Convention   32
Knox, John   55–56

laity   32–33
   see also baptism
Lateran council, Fourth   4, 26
Leidrad of Lyons   51–53
Lent   70, 72
liturgy
   see baptism
Lord's Prayer   48, 55, 68
Lord's supper   2, 3–4, 26, 68, 83, 85, 88, 93
Luther, Martin   11, 19–20, 54
   Baptism Booklet, 1523   54
   Baptism Booklet, 1526   54
   Concerning Rebaptism   20
   Defence of All the Articles   19–20
   Large Catechism   96–97
   Small Catechism   69, 96
Lutheranism   4, 5, 12, 13, 16, 54, 56, 73, 86, 96–97

Magdeburg *Agenda*   54
martyrdom   29, 64
mass   3, 83
Methodism   86, 100
midwives   26–27

Nazarene Church   ix–x, 16
Nicaea, council   64
   see also Creeds

Ordo Romanus XI   71–72
Origen   66
original sin
   see sin
Oxford Movement   88

paedobaptism *passim*
parents   13, 16, 35, 41–42, 43,
    50–51, 54–61, 73, 80, 101
Paris   48
Pascha   76
patristic
    see Fathers
Pentecost   8, 64, 69, 70
Pentecostalism   9
Peter Martyr Vermigli   45
pistos
    see believers
Presbyterian   12
Presbyterian Church (USA)   16
profession of faith
    see faith
Protestants, Protestantism   29, 31
Puritans   81

quam primum   25, 81
questions
    see baptism

reductionism, baptismal   viii, 23–25, 87–88
Reformation, Reformers   viii, 3, 7, 12, 19, 23, 24, 26, 29, 30, 45, 46,   54–57, 69, 73, 90, 94, 100
Reformed churches, tradition   4, 12, 54–57, 97–99
regeneration   24, 80, 94, 99, 100
Rite of Christian Initiation of Adults   10, 78–80, 82
Roman Catholicism   9, 10, 14, 30, 78–79, 83, 100
    rite of infant baptism (1969)   59, 62, 80–81, 82
Rome, church of   38, 47–48

Rome, Roman Empire   12, 38

sacrament   50–52, 87–88
Sarum Manual   27, 46, 49, 68–71, 72
Scotland   4, 5, 13
    see also Church of Scotland, Special Commission
Scots Confession   95
Scripture alone   23
scrutinies   71–72
Second Helvetic Confession   24, 98
Senarius   47
sin, original   7, 25
Southern Baptists   35
Special Commission on Baptism   18
sponsors (godparents)   8, 13, 35, 43, 44, 45, 50–62
Strasbourg   12, 54–55
Sweden   13, 16, 28, 86

Tertullian   66, 68, 74–75
    Apology   74
    Baptism   75
thanksgiving (for adoption, birth)   59
Theodulf of Orleans   49–50
Thirtynine Articles   94–95
Thomas Aquinas   26
Tractarians   88
Trinity   26

United States of America   13

Vatican   4
    council, Second   10, 25, 78–81
Vermigli, Peter Martyr   45

Waldensians 26
Westminster Assembly 24
　　Confession of Faith 24, 98–99

Zürich 56
Zwingli, Ulrich 56–57

The Didsbury Lecture Series

1979   F.F. Bruce
Men and Movements in the Primitive Church

1980   I.H. Marshall
Last Supper and Lord's Supper
ISBN: 1-84227-307-8

1981   J. Atkinson
Martin Luther: Prophet to the Church Catholic

1982   T.F. Torrance
The Mediation of Christ

1983   C.K. Barrett
Church Ministry and Sacraments

1984   A.R.G. Deasley
The Shape of Qumran Theology
ISBN: 0-85364-786-0

1985   D. Guthrie
The Relevance of John's Apocalypse

1986   A. Skevington-Wood
Revelation and Reason

1987   A.F. Walls
The Making of the Nineteenth-Century Missionary

1988   M.D. Hooker
Not Ashamed of the Gospel

1989   R.E. Clements
Wisdom in Theology

1990   C.E. Gunton
Christ and Creation
ISBN: 1-84227-305-1

1991   J.D.G. Dunn
Christian Liberty

1992   P. Bassett
A Redefinition of Heresy

1993   D.J.A Clines
The Bible Today

1994   J.B. Torrance
Worship, Community and the Triune God of Grace

1995   R.T. France
Women in the Church's Ministry

1996   R. Bauckham
God Crucified: Monotheism and Christology in the New Testament
ISBN: 0-85364-944-8

1997   H.G.M. Williamson
Variation on a Theme: King, Messiah and Servant in the book of Isaiah
ISBN: 0-85364-870-0

1998   D. Bebbington
Holiness in Nineteenth-Century England
ISBN: 0-85634-981-2

1999   L.W. Hurtado
At the Origins of Christian Worship: The Context and Character of Earliest Christian Devotion
ISBN: 0-85364-992-8

2000   C.H. Pinnock
Most Moved Mover: A Theology of God's Openness
ISBN: 1-84227-014-1

2001   R.P. Gordon
Holy Land, Holy City: Sacred Geography and the Interpretation of the Bible
ISBN: 1-84227-277-2

2002   H. McGonigle
Wesley as a Practical Theologian
(Title to be confirmed, forthcoming)

2003   D. F. Wright
What has Infant Baptism done to Baptism? An enquiry at the end of Christendom
ISBN: 1-84227-357-4

2004   S. Smalley
Hope For Ever: The Christian View of Life and Death
(Forthcoming)

2005   N.T. Wright

2006   A. Sell
Non-Conformist Theologians
(Title to be confirmed, forthcoming)

For a full list of the Didsbury Lectures titles
see the end of this book.

Holy Land, Holy City
*Sacred Geography and the
Interpretation of the Bible*

Robert P. Gordon

ISBN: 1-84227-277-2

What connections exist between the physical geography of Israel and the spirituality of biblical faith? How was the physical space conceived as sacred space?

In a wide-ranging study Professor Robert Gordon leads the readers from the Garden of Eden to Jerusalem, from Genesis through the Psalms and the gospels to Revelation, and onwards through the patristic period, the Middle Ages and the nineteenth and twentieth centuries. Chapters one to four concentrate on Old Testament texts and themes relating to the 'holy land, holy city'. History, as well as geography plays a part here. Gordon shows in particular how topography of Jerusalem and its environment have been used in diverse ways in the spirituality of Jews and Christians over the centuries.

Chapters five through to nine begin with 'The Geography of Golgatha' and progress into the prophetic envisioning of the end-time pilgrimage of the nations to Jerusalem. The vexed question of land disputes between Israel and the Palestinians is also considered. *Holy Land, Holy City* offers a current and contemporary reading of sacred geography in the Bible.

Subject-related titles
Relaunched as part of the Paternoster Digital Library

Baptism in the New Testament

G.R. Beasley-Murray

ISBN: 1-84227-300-0

Baptism is still front-page news – as it was more than forty years ago when this authoritative survey of New Testament teaching about Baptism was first published. *Baptism in the New Testament* considers the Old Testament and Judaistic background to baptism as well as discussing the rise and significance of infant baptism.

Studies in Baptist History and Thought

More Than a Symbol (vol. 2)
The British Baptist Recovery of Baptismal Sacramentalism

Stanley K. Fowler

ISBN: 1-84227-052-4

Fowler surveys the entire scope of British Baptist literature from the seventeenth-century pioneers onwards, showing that the interpretation of baptism as a mere symbol bearing witness to a previously completed conversion experience is inadequate.

Baptism and the Baptists (vol. 3)
Theology and Practice in Twentieth-Century Britain

Anthony R. Cross

ISBN: 0-85364-959-6

At a time of renewed interest in baptism, *Baptism and the Baptists* is a detailed study of twentieth-century baptismal theology and practice and the factors which have influenced their development.